A Commentary on the United Nations Convention on the Rights of the Child

Editors

André Alen, Johan Vande Lanotte, Eugeen Verhellen, Fiona Ang, Eva Berghmans and Mieke Verheyde

Article 28

The Right to Education

By

Mieke Verheyde

Researcher at the Human Rights Centre, Ghent University, Belgium

MARTINUS NIJHOFF PUBLISHERS
LEIDEN • BOSTON
2006

This book is printed on acid-free paper.

A Cataloging-in-Publication record for this book is available from the Library of Congress.

Cite as: M. Verheyde, "Article 28: The Right to Education", in: A. Alen, J. Vande Lanotte, E. Verhellen, F. Ang, E. Berghmans and M. Verheyde (Eds.) *A Commentary on the United Nations Convention on the Rights of the Child* (Martinus Nijhoff Publishers, Leiden, 2006).

ISSN 1574-8626
ISBN 90-04-14729-2

Koninklijke Brill NV incorporates the imprints Brill Academic Publishers, Martinus Nijhoff Publishers and VSP.

Cover image by Nadia, 1½ years old.

http://www.brill.nl

Article 28

The Right to Education

CONTENTS

LIST OF ABBREVIATIONS

CCPR	International Covenant on Civil and Political Rights
CEDAW	International Convention on the Elimination of All Forms of Discrimination against Women
CERD	International Convention on the Elimination of All Forms of Racial Discrimination
CESCR	International Covenant on Economic, Social and Cultural Rights
CESCR Committee	UN Committee on Economic, Social and Cultural Rights
CRC	International Convention on the Rights of the Child
CRC Committee	UN Committee on the Rights of the Child
ECHR	European Convention on Human Rights
ECmHR	European Commission on Human Rights
ECtHR	European Court of Human Rights
EU	European Union
UDHR	Universal Declaration of Human Rights
UN	United Nations
UNESCO	United Nations Educational, Scientific and Cultural Organisation

AUTHOR BIOGRAPHY

Mieke Verheyde is a Belgian researcher at the Human Rights Centre of Ghent University (Belgium). She is involved in an interdisciplinary inter-university research project on the UN Convention on the Rights of the Child and conducts comparative research on the protection of children's rights by the European Court of Human Rights and the US Supreme Court. Previously, she worked for two years as a researcher on women's rights issues in the Cabinet of the Belgian federal minister of employment and labour, and as a member of the Equal Opportunities Department of the Belgian federal ministry of employment and labour. She studied law at the University of Leuven (Belgium), obtained an LL.M. at the University of Stellenbosch (South Africa) and a European Master's Degree in Human Rights and Democratisation at the University of Padova (Italy).

TEXT OF ARTICLE 28

Article 28	Article 28
1. States Parties recognize the right of the child to education and with a view to achieving this right progressively and on the basis of equal opportunity, they shall, in particular:	*1. Les Etats parties reconnaissent le droit de l'enfant à l'éducation, et en particulier, en vue d'assurer l'exercice de ce droit progressivement et sur la base de l'égalité des chances:*
(a) Make primary education compulsory and available free to all;	*(a) Ils rendent l'enseignement primaire obligatoire et gratuit pour tous;*
(b) Encourage the development of different forms of secondary education, including general and vocational education, make them available and accessible to every child and take appropriate measures such as the introduction of free education and offering financial assistance in case of need;	*(b) Ils encouragent l'organisation de différentes formes d'enseignement secondaire, tant général que professionnel, les rendent ouvertes et accessibles à tout enfant, et prennent des mesures appropriées, telles que l'instauration de la gratuité de l'enseignement et l'offre d'une aide financière en cas de besoin;*
(c) Make higher education accessible to all on the basis of capacity by every appropriate means;	*(c) Ils assurent à tous l'accès à l'enseignement supérieur, en fonction des capacités de chacun, par tous les moyens appropriés;*
(d) Make educational and vocational information and guidance available and accessible to all children;	*(d) Ils rendent ouvertes et accessibles à tout enfant l'information et l'orientation scolaires et professionnelles;*
(e) Take measures to encourage regular attendance at schools and the reduction of drop-out rates.	*(e) Ils prennent des mesures pour encourager la régularité de la fréquentation scolaire et la réduction des taux d'abandon scolaire.*

2. States Parties shall take all appropriate measures to ensure that school discipline is administered in a manner consistent with the child's human dignity and in conformity with the present Convention.

3. States Parties shall promote and encourage international cooperation in matters relating to education, in particular with a view to contributing to the elimination of ignorance and illiteracy throughout the world and facilitating access to scientific and technical knowledge and modern teaching methods. In this regard, particular account shall be taken of the needs of developing countries.

2. Les Etats parties prennent toutes les mesures appropriées pour veiller à ce que la discipline scolaire soit appliquée d'une manière compatible avec la dignité de l'enfant en tant qu'être humain et conformément à la présente Convention.

3. Les Etats parties favorisent et encouragent la coopération internationale dans le domaine de l'éducation, en vue notamment de contribuer à éliminer l'ignorance et l'analphabétisme dans le monde et de faciliter l'accès aux connaissances scientifiques et techniques et aux méthodes d'enseignement modernes. A cet égard, il est tenu particulièrement compte des besoins des pays en développement.

CHAPTER ONE

INTRODUCTION*

1. The present contribution comprises an attempt to identify the content of the right to education and the corresponding State obligations enshrined in Article 28 of the Convention on the Rights of the Child.[1] Article 28 is not the CRC's only provision on education. Article 29, pertaining to the aims of education in its first paragraph and the freedom of individuals and bodies to establish educational institutions in its second paragraph, is the CRC's other core provision on education. Both articles are interlinked and should be read together: the right to receive education does not only guarantee access to education but also implies that the aims of education must be achieved.[2] The education rights enshrined in these core provisions can be categorised in several ways. One possible categorisation is to put the education rights in the framework of the three generations of human rights.[3] The right to receive education on the basis of equal opportunity (Article 28(1)) is a second generation right (according to some, a social right,[4] according

* September 2004. With special thanks to Mr Duncan Wilson for his useful comments.

[1] Hereinafter referred to as 'the CRC' or 'the Convention'. The Convention was adopted on 20 November 1989 and entered into force 2 September 1990. As at September 2004, the CRC has been signed and ratified by 192 States, which makes it almost universal (Somalia and the United States are the only States that signed the Convention without ratifying it).

[2] M. Mehedi, *The Realisation of Economic, Social and Cultural Rights. The Realisation of the Right to Education, including Education in Human Rights—The Content of the Right to Education* (UN Doc. E/CN.4/Sub.2/1999/10, 1999), para. 40. *Cf.* also *infra* No. 19.

[3] See J. Delbrück, 'The Right to Education as an International Human Right', *German Yearbook of International Law* 35, 1992, p. 104; M. Mehedi, *o.c.* (note 2), para. 51; M. Nowak, 'The Right to Education', in: A. Eide, C. Krause, A. Rosas (eds.), *Economic, Social and Cultural Rights* (Dordrecht/Boston/London, Martinus Nijhoff Publishers, 2001), pp. 252–255 and K. Tomaševski, *Right to Education Primer 3: Human rights obligations: making education available, accessible, acceptable and adaptable* (Lund, Raoul Wallenberg Institute, 2001), p. 9. See also Coomans, who speaks about 'the social aspect' and 'the freedom aspect' of the right to education: A.P.M. Coomans, *De internationale bescherming van het recht op onderwijs* (Leiden, Stichting NJCM Boekerij, 1992), pp. 45–46 and F. Coomans, 'In search of the core content of the right to education', in: A. Chapman and S. Russell (eds.), *Core obligations: Building a Framework for Economic, Social and Cultural Rights* (Antwerp/Oxford/New York, Intersentia, 2002), p. 220.

[4] *E.g.* J. Delbrück, 'The Right to Education as an International Human Right', *l.c.* (note 3), p. 104; A.P.M. Coomans, *De internationale bescherming van het recht op onderwijs*, *o.c.* (note 3), p. 53; F. Coomans, 'In search of the core content of the right to education', *l.c.* (note 3), p. 220; and M. Mehedi, *o.c.* (note 2), para. 52.

to others, a cultural right).[5] Article 29(2) regarding the freedom of individuals and bodies to establish educational institutions is an example of the 'civil right' category. Also Article 28(2), safeguarding a humane disciplinary system in schools, is mainly of a civil rights' nature. Article 28(3), promoting international co-operation in the field of education falls as a so-called 'solidarity right' into the category of third generation of human rights.[6] Another possible classification of the CRC's education rights is to place them under three headings: the right TO education, IN education and THROUGH education.[7] The right TO education entails the provisions regarding the practical organisation of education (Article 28(1)) and the organisation as to its content (Article 29(1)). The rights IN education are the protection rights entrenched in the CRC (including Article 28(2)) as well as the several participation rights of the child. Both should be respected in school settings. The notion 'rights THROUGH education' refers to the indirect implementation of the CRC and other human rights standards by means of human rights education (Article 29(1)(b)).

Given the holistic nature of the CRC, Article 28 should not only be read together with Article 29 but also with several other articles of the Convention. In this respect, Article 4 is of relevance with regard to the implementation of the education rights. Also Articles 2 (general non-discrimination principle), 3 (the best interests of the child), 6 (right to life, survival and development), and 12 (the view of the child)—identified as the general principles of the Convention—should be taken into consideration when implementing education rights.[8] Other Articles of the Convention closely related are *inter alia*: Articles 13 till 17 containing provisions on participation, Article 19(1) protecting the child from all forms of maltreatment perpetrated by among others teachers, Article 23(3) ensuring effective education for disabled children, Article 24(2)(e) concerning health education, Article 30 on

[5] *E.g.* A. Eide, 'Cultural Rights and Individual Human Rights', in: A. Eide, C. Krause, A. Rosas (eds.), *Economic, Social and Cultural Rights* (Dordrecht/Boston/London, Martinus Nijhoff Publishers, 2001), p. 292 and M. Nowak, 'The Right to Education', *l.c.* (note 3), p. 253.

[6] M. Mehedi, *o.c.* (note 2), paras. 51 and 74; and M. Nowak, 'The Right to Education', *l.c.* (note 3), pp. 254–255.

[7] K. Tomaševski, *Right to Education Primer 3: Human rights obligations: making education available, accessible, acceptable and adaptable*, *o.c.* (note 3), p. 12; L. Cattrijsse, 'Children's Rights and Education: The Right TO, IN and THROUGH Education: three interrelated imperatives', in: E. Verhellen (ed.), *Understanding Children's Rights 2000*—No. 6 (Gent, Children's Rights Centre, 2001), pp. 619–640 and E. Verhellen, *Convention on the Rights of the Child* (Leuven-Apeldoorn, Garant, 2000), pp. 105–111.

[8] CRC Committee, *General Guidelines regarding the form and the contents of the periodic reports* (UN Doc. CRC/C/58, 1996), para. 106.

the rights of children belonging tot a minority or an indigenous population, Article 32 regarding child labour and Articles 44(6) and 43 regarding human rights education.

2. For the purposes of the present text, the analysis of the right to education in its several dimensions is structured along the text of Article 28. A first part under Chapter 3 ('Scope of Article 28') therefore deals with the first paragraph of Article 28, guaranteeing the right to receive education on the basis of equal opportunities and indirectly also the freedom to choose education (No. 8–45). A second part focuses on the second paragraph of Article 28, concerning the right to a humane disciplinary system (No. 46–50). In a last part, the third paragraph of Article 28 on international cooperation in education is examined (No. 51–53).

3. For the purposes of interpreting the provisions in Article 28, use has been made of the interpretation rules, laid down in the Vienna Convention on the Law of Treaties,[9] supplemented with the findings of the UN Committee on the Rights of the Child[10] and relevant doctrine on the subject.

In the first place, the interpretation rules of the Vienna Convention on the Law of Treaties have been applied. Article 31(1) of this Convention states that a treaty should be interpreted 'in accordance with the ordinary meaning to be given to the term of the treaty in their context and in the light of its object and purpose'. Therefore the wordings of Article 28, put in their relation to other provisions in the Convention and the preamble have been given primary consideration. Also equivalent provisions in other international and regional human rights conventions were taken into account. Justification for this reliance follows from the preamble of the CRC and Article 31(3)(c) of the Vienna Convention. The preamble of the CRC recalls the basic principles of the United Nations and specific provisions of relevant human rights treaties and proclamations, such as the Universal Declaration of Human Rights (1948) and both International Covenants on Human Rights (1966). Article 31(3)(c) of the Vienna Convention states that 'there shall be taken into account, together with the context any relevant rules of international law applicable in the relations between the parties'.

---

[9] Articles 31–33 of the Vienna Convention on The Law of Treaties, adopted on 23 May 1969, entered into force 27 January 1980. The general rules of interpretation enshrined in this Convention are also applicable to human rights conventions: See R. Bernhardt, 'Thoughts on the interpretation of human-rights treaties', in: F. Matscher and H. Petzold, *Protecting Human Rights: Studies in honour of Gérard J. Wiarda* (Köln, Heymanns, 1988), p. 70.

[10] Hereinafter referred to as 'the CRC Committee'.

Moreover, reliance upon the interpretations of other UN human rights treaties has been promoted within the UN treaty system itself.[11] It should be mentioned that there exist divided opinions regarding the relevance of regional standards as to the interpretation of international provisions. Some commentators speculate that this could lead to improperly universalising the regional standards.[12] Others seem to recognise that the 'good practice' at the regional level regarding the protection and promotion of the child's education rights may reconfirm the obligations of States at the international level.[13] The latter position is followed in this contribution. In line with Article 32 of the Vienna Convention on the Law of Treaties, also the *Travaux Préparatoires* were sometimes drawn upon as a supplementary means of interpretation to clarify the scope of Article 28 of the CRC.

In the second place, the findings of the CRC Committee as well as of other UN treaty bodies[14] have been drawn upon. Especially the general comments and the concluding observations of the CRC Committee are of a high ranking in interpreting Article 28 of the CRC. Although neither type of decisions are internationally binding, they have been treated as an authoritative interpretation as both contain the view of the CRC Committee—which can be considered as the most authoritative body monitoring the Convention[15]—as a whole.[16] General comments are summaries of the Committee's experience

[11] Although some treaty bodies took a restrictive view in this regard, the General Assembly, the Human Rights Commission as well as legal doctrine strongly advocate in favour of a consistent interpretation of human rights standards: I. Boerefijn, *The Reporting Procedure under the Covenant on Civil and Political Rights: Practice and Procedures of the Human Rights Committee* (Antwerpen-Groningen-Oxford, Intersentia-Hart, 1999), pp. 162, 165, 167–168 and 296–297.

[12] B. Abramson, 'Book Review: Sharon Detrick: *A Commentary on the United Nations Convention on the Rights of the Child.* Martinus Nijhoff: The Hague, Boston, London, 1999, 790p.', *The International Journal of Children's Rights* 9, 2001, No. 1, p. 65.

[13] As far as the interpretation of the CCPR is concerned, see M. Nowak, *U.N. Covenant on Civil and Political Rights—CCPR Commentary* (Kehl/Strasbourg/Arlington, N.P. Engel Publisher, 1993), p. XXIII, para. 18; with regard to the interpretation of the CRC, see M. Nowak, 'The Right to Education', *l.c.* (note 3), p. 266.

[14] And especially the findings of the UN Committee on Economic, Social and Cultural Rights. Hereafter referred to as 'the CESCR Committee'.

[15] The Committee was established by the drafters of the Convention, See Article 43(1) of the CRC.

[16] The moral authority of general comments has been stressed by some scholars. As far as the general comments of the Human Rights Committee are concerned, see I. Boerefijn, *The Reporting Procedure under the Covenant on Civil and Political Rights, o.c.* (note 11), pp. 294 and 300; Y. Iwasawa, 'The domestic impact of international human rights standards: the Japanese experience', in: Ph. Alston and J. Crawford (eds.), *The Future of UN Human Rights Treaty Monitoring* (Cambridge, Cambridge University Press, 2000), pp. 258–259 and M. Nowak, *U.N. Covenant on Civil and Political Rights—CCPR Commentary, o.c.* (note 13), p. XXIV, para. 21 and p. 576. On the moral authority of concluding observations: See I. Boerefijn, 'The Human

gained so far through the examination of State reports, and are directed to all States Parties. Concluding observations are merely country-specific and should therefore in principle be given less weight than general comments. Reference has however especially been made to recurring observations, which are thus of a more general nature and most probably will constitute the basis of future general comments. In a few cases, also the recommendations, made by the CRC Committee at the end of a general discussion day on a specific topic, and its reporting guidelines were taken into account for some questions of interpretation. Also the practice of other UN Treaty bodies has been used to that purpose. Especially the holdings of the CESCR Committee were relied upon as Article 28 has largely been drawn along the lines of the equivalent provision in the CESCR.

Finally, the relevant legal doctrine, including the findings of the Special Rapporteur on the right to education, has been consulted in the identification of the scope of Article 28 of the CRC.

Rights Committee's Concluding Observations', in: M. Castermans-Holleman, F. Van Hoof and J. Smith (eds.), *The role of the nation-state in the 21st century, foreign policy, human rights, international organisations* (The Hague, Kluwer, 1998), pp. 232 and 248; and I. Boerefijn, *The Reporting Procedure under the Covenant on Civil and Political Rights, o.c.* (note 11), pp. 303–304.

CHAPTER TWO

COMPARISON WITH RELATED INTERNATIONAL HUMAN RIGHTS STANDARDS

4. Given the double dimension of education as both a human right in itself and an indispensable means of realizing other human rights,[17] the right to education is abundantly guaranteed in several global and regional, general and specific human rights instruments.[18]

The main universal human rights instruments recognising the right to education are: Article 26 of the Universal Declaration of Human Rights (1948),[19] Principle 7 of the Declaration of the Rights of the Child (1959), the Convention against Discrimination in Education (1960),[20] Articles 13–14 of the International Covenant on Economic, Social and Cultural Rights (1966),[21] and Articles 28 and 29 of the CRC.

Other universal instruments address specific aspects of the right to education or protect the right to education of particularly vulnerable groups. These include *inter alia* Article 22 of the Convention relating to the Status of Refugees (1951),[22] Article 5(e)(v) of the Convention on the Elimination of all Forms of Racial Discrimination (1965),[23] Article 18(4) of the International Covenant on Civil and Political Rights (1966),[24] Principle 6 of the Declaration

---

[17] See on this issue among others A. Chapman, *Violations of the right to education* (UN Doc. E/C.12/1998/19, 1998), para. 1; F. Coomans, 'In search of the core content of the right to education', *l.c.* (note 3), pp. 219–220; M. Mehedi, *o.c.* (note 2), paras. 1–4; K. Tomaševski, *Annual Report of the Special Rapporteur on the Right to Education 2000/9* (UN Doc. E/CN.4/2001/52, 2001), paras. 11–14 and 79; and CESCR Committee, *General Comment No. 13 on the Right to Education* (UN Doc. E/C.12/1999/10, 1999), para. 1.

[18] For an overview on international law regarding the right to education, see D. Hodgson, 'The international human right to education and education concerning human rights', *The international Journal of Children's Rights* 4, 1996, pp. 239–251; and G. Van Bueren, *The International Law on the Rights of the Child* (The Hague, Martinus Nijhoff Publishers, 1998), pp. 232–261.

[19] Universal Declaration on Human Rights, adopted on 10 December 1948. Hereinafter referred to as UDHR.

[20] UNESCO Convention against Discrimination in Education, adopted on 14 December 1960, entered into force 22 May 1962.

[21] International Covenant on Economic, Social and Cultural Rights, adopted on 16 December 1966, entered into force 3 January 1976. Hereinafter referred to as CESCR.

[22] Convention relating to the Status of Refugees, adopted on 28 July 1951, entered into force 22 April 1954.

[23] International Convention on the Elimination of All Forms of Racial Discrimination, adopted on 21 December 1965, entered into force 4 January 1969. Hereinafter referred to as CERD.

[24] International Covenant on Civil and Political Rights, adopted on 16 December 1966, entered into force 23 March 1976. Hereinafter referred to as CCPR.

on the Rights of Disabled Persons (1975),[25] Article 10 of the Convention on the Elimination of All Forms of Discrimination Against Women (1979),[26] Article 30 of the International Convention on the Protection of the Rights of all Migrant Workers and Their Families (1990),[27] and Article 4(3) of the Declaration on the Rights of Persons Belonging to National or Ethnic, Religious and Linguistic Minorities (1992).[28]

At the regional level, the main instruments containing the right to education are: Article XII of the American Declaration of the Rights and Duties of Man (1948),[29] Article 2 of Protocol No. 1 of the European Convention for the Protection of Human Rights and Fundamental Freedoms (1952),[30] Article 17 of the African Charter on Human and Peoples' Rights (1981),[31] Article 13 of the Additional Protocol of San Salvador to the American Convention on Human Rights in the Area of Economic, Social and Cultural Rights (1988),[32] Article 11 of the African Charter on the Rights and Welfare of the Child (1990),[33] Article 34 of the Arab Charter on Human Rights (1994),[34] Article 17 of the European Social Charter (1996),[35] and Article 14 of the EU Charter of Fundamental Rights (2000).[36] Regional instruments addressing specific aspects include among others Article 8 of the European Charter for Regional or Minority Languages (1998),[37] and Article 14 of the Framework Convention for the Protection of National Minorities (1998).[38]

---

[25] Declaration on the Rights of Disabled Persons, adopted on 9 December 1975.

[26] International Convention on the Elimination of All Forms of Discrimination against Women, adopted on 18 December 1979, entered into force 3 September 1981. Hereinafter referred to as CEDAW.

[27] The International Convention on the Protection of the Rights of All Migrant Workers and Members of their Families, adopted on18 December 1990, entered into force 1 July 2003.

[28] Declaration on the Rights of Persons Belonging to National or Ethnic, Religious and Linguistic Minorities, adopted on 18 December 1992.

[29] American Declaration of the Rights and Duties of Man, adopted on 2 May 1948.

[30] Protocol No. 1 of the European Convention for the Protection of Human Rights and Fundamental Freedoms (hereinafter referred to as ECHR), adopted on 20 March 1952, entered into force 18 May 1954.

[31] African Charter on Human and Peoples' Rights, adopted on 26 June 1981, entered into force 21 October 1986.

[32] Additional Protocol of San Salvador to the American Convention on Human Rights in the Area of Economic, Social and Cultural Rights—'Protocol of San Salvador', adopted on 17 November 1988, entered into force 16 November 1999.

[33] African Charter on the Rights and Welfare of the Child, adopted on 11 July 1990, entered into force 29 November 1999.

[34] Arab Charter on Human Rights, adopted on 15 September 1994.

[35] Revised European Social Charter, adopted on 3 May 1996, entered into force 1 July 1999.

[36] Charter of Fundamental Rights of the European Union, adopted on 7 December 2000.

[37] European Charter for Regional or Minority Languages, adopted by the Council of Europe on 5 November 1992, entered into force 1 March 1998.

[38] Framework Convention for the Protection of National Minorities, adopted by the Council of Europe on 1 February 1995, entered into force 1 February 1998.

5. Article 28 of the CRC repeats most of the education rights guaranteed in the above mentioned International Bill of Rights and main regional instruments. The article is in particular phrased in line with Article 13 of the CESCR. The CRC does, however, not merely copy the existing international education rights law but inserts a new dimension to it: education should be child-centred and child-friendly in both a protective and an empowering way. Protective, in the sense that it protects children against an inhumane disciplinary system in schools, against child labour which may impede the education of the child, and it contains some specific protection measures ensuring the education of especially vulnerable children. Empowering, in the sense that the provisions reflect an impetus for more emancipation, increased self-determination and responsibility of children and a guiding rather than decisive role for the parents in education. The CRC hence reconceptualised the existing international education rights law from the child's perspective. The text of Article 28, referring to 'the child' as holder of the right to education and omitting a reference to the traditionally recognised parental right to respect for their religious and philosophical convictions in the education of their children, clearly proves this new dimension.

6. In addition to the new dimension it puts in existing education rights, the CRC broadens the arsenal of binding international provisions on the right to education. Firstly, Article 28(1)(d) imposes a duty on the States Parties to make educational and vocational information and guidance available and accessible to all. Secondly, Article 28(1)(e) requires that the States Parties should take measures to encourage regular school attendance and the reduction of school dropout rates. Thirdly, Article 28(2) expressly enshrines the principle that school discipline should be administered in a manner consistent with the child's human dignity and in conformity with the international rights of the child. The article has the additional value of not only prohibiting disciplinary measures, which constitute torture or are cruel, inhuman or degrading, but also requiring that these measures should be administered in accordance with the child's dignity and human rights, including participation rights. Fourthly, Articles 28(1), 5, 14(2) and 12 could be read together as guaranteeing that participation of children in decisions that help ensure their education is in conformity with *their own* religious and moral convictions.[39] Finally, Article 28(3) contains the most comprehensive and explicit call in an internationally binding human rights document to international cooperation in matters relating to education.

---

[39] G. Van Bueren, *The International Law on the Rights of the Child*, *o.c.* (note 18), p. 243.

7. Article 28 of the CRC has, however, also a weak point: it does not always offer the strongest international protection in education. The CESCR imposes stronger obligations to the States Parties at the three levels of education.

At primary level, the States have under Article 13(2)(a) of the CESCR a clear and unconditional obligation to immediately ensure free and compulsory education. Article 28(1)(a) only obliges States to realise this in a progressive manner. Furthermore, the CESCR imposes in its Article 14 an obligation on the States, which at the time of becoming a party have not been able to secure compulsory and free primary education to undertake, within two years to work out and adopt a detailed plan of action for the progressive implementation, within a reasonable number of years, to be fixed in the plan, of the principle of compulsory education free of charge for all. The CRC does not contain a similar obligation of conduct, which would facilitate international monitoring of the implementation of the education rights and hence their realisation.

At the level of secondary education, the terms of Article 13(2)(b) of the CESCR reflect an obligation 'to develop' different forms of secondary education, which is stronger than the obligation 'to encourage the development of' different forms of secondary education under Article 28(1)(b). Further, the term 'in particular' in Article 13(2)(b) of the CESCR reveals a clear obligation to take steps towards the realisation of cost-free secondary education. The notion 'such as' in Article 28(1)(b) of the CRC, on the other hand, refers to the introduction of cost-free secondary education merely as an example of how education could be made accessible to all children. States Parties under the CRC have no obligation to make secondary education free of costs if they can make secondary education accessible to all children by other means.

At the level of higher education, Article 13(2)(c) of the CESCR enshrines an obligation to introduce free education, whilst under Article 28(1)(c) of the CRC States are not obliged to organise free higher education nor to take some steps in this direction.

However, these gaps in Article 28 of the CRC may be filled by the saving clause enshrined in Article 41 of the CRC. This article provides that, if any standard set in national law or other applicable international instruments are higher than those of this Convention, it is the higher standard that applies.

CHAPTER THREE

SCOPE OF ARTICLE 28

1. *Article 28(1): The Right to Receive Education on the basis of Equal Opportunities and the Freedom to Choose Education*

1.1 *The Right to Receive Education*

8. The right to receive education constitutes the core of the right to education under international human rights law.[40] The first paragraph of Article 28 guarantees this right by imposing positive obligations on the States Parties to develop and maintain an educational system in order to provide education to all children at specific levels (primary, secondary and higher), and, according to the level, cost-free and compulsory.

1.1.1 *The Definition of Education*

9. Like any other international human rights instrument, the CRC does not provide for a clear definition of education. Usually, international legal instruments use the term 'education' in a double sense: a) education as the provision of basic skills, and b) education as the development of the intellectual, spiritual, and emotional potential of the young person or in other words the broader development of his or her personality.[41] Article 28(1) undoubtedly refers to education in both senses. General as well as vocational and professional basic skills are to be provided by the States Parties. The CRC Committee stresses that the notion 'basic skills' does not only include

---

[40] M. Nowak, 'The Right to Education' *l.c.* (note 3), p. 255.

[41] J. Delbrück, 'The Right to Education as an International Human Right', *l.c.* (note 3), pp. 94 and 99.

Outside the context of international human rights obligations, the concept of education may have a broader meaning: UNESCO defined the term 'education' as implying 'the entire process of social life by means of which individuals and social groups learn to develop consciously within, and for the benefit of, the national and international communities, the whole of their personal capacities, attitudes, aptitudes and knowledge. This process is not limited to any specific activities'. (Article 1(a) of the UNESCO *Recommendation concerning education for international understanding, co-operation and peace and education relating to human rights and fundamental freedoms*, adopted in Paris on 19 November 1974).

'literacy and numeracy but also life skills such as the ability to make well-balanced decisions; to resolve conflicts in a non-violent manner; and to develop a healthy lifestyle, good social relationships and responsibility, critical thinking, creative talents, and other abilities which give children the tools needed to pursue their options in life'.[42] These aspects refer to the second, broader aspect of the term 'education'. That the notion 'education' under the CRC should be understood in this broader sense is confirmed by a combined reading of Articles 28(1) and 29(1) of the CRC, containing the extensive goals of education to be achieved throughout the curriculum. Accordingly, 'education' under Article 28(1) should be understood as the process of developing the child's personality, talents, mental and physical abilities; developing the child's respect for human rights, fundamental freedoms and the maintenance of peace, respect for his or her parents, national values of his or her country and those of other civilizations; developing the child's ability to participate in a free society in the spirit of mutual tolerance; and developing the child's respect for other civilizations, cultures, religions, sexes and for the natural environment.

The text of Article 28(1) is also silent about the question whether Article 28(1) refers to both formal and non-formal education or only to formal education. Formal education is structured, chronologically graded instruction, given in an educational institution. Non-formal education is an organised educational activity outside the established formal classroom system,[43] such as village, community-based, or open air schooling.[44] The findings of the CRC Committee make believe that Article 28(1) refers to both formal and non-formal education. In its reporting guidelines, the Committee asks the States to indicate any system of non-formal education in their country.[45] In its concluding observations to the States reports, the Committee often recommends governments to set up non-formal structures and to use informal educational programmes, especially when children are in the impossibility

---

[42] CRC Committee, *General Comment No. 1 on the Aims of Education* (UN Doc. CRC/GC/2001/1, 2001), para. 9. Similar definitions can be found in Article 1 of the World Declaration on Education for All, adopted in 1990 in Jomtien (Thailand), in: *World Education Forum, The Dakar Framework for Action, Education for All: Meeting our Collective Commitments* (Paris, UNESCO, 2000), p. 75; and in Article 3 of the Dakar Framework for Action, adopted in 2000 in Dakar (Senegal), in: *World Education Forum, The Dakar Framework for Action, Education for All: Meeting our Collective Commitments* (Paris, UNESCO, 2000), p. 8.

[43] L. Cattrijsse, 'Children's Rights and Education: The Right TO, IN and THROUGH Education: three interrelated imperatives', *l.c.* (note 7), p. 621.

[44] F. Coomans, 'In search of the core content of the right to education', *l.c.* (note 3), p. 226.

[45] CRC Committee, *General Guidelines regarding the form and the contents of the periodic reports* (UN Doc. CRC/C/58, 1996), para. 106.

to attend regular schools, such as working children and street children.[46] Further, States are recommended to ensure that the quality of non-formal education schemes is monitored and guaranteed, and that working and other children who participate in such schemes are integrated into mainstream education.[47] The CRC Committee thus encourages the State Party to harmonize the formal and non-formal education systems.[48] The inclusion of non-formal education in the notion 'education' has been reconfirmed by some scholars.[49] Despite the fact that other scholars tend not to agree with this point of view, one could conclude that the notion 'education' in Article 28(1) refers to both formal an non-formal education.[50] States Parties under the CRC should therefore ensure that these non-formal programmes share the same standards of learning applied to schools and comply with the human rights requirements in education, such as the principle of equal opportunity.

10. Also in terms of duration the notion 'education' in Article 28(1) has not been defined. Neither the beginning nor the end of education is indicated. It thus remains open at what age education has to start. It is not clear whether States have an obligation to organise pre-primary education. During the drafting of the Convention, the proposals to guarantee overall care for the child of pre-school age were not adopted.[51] The right to pre-primary education is also absent in the majority of other binding universal and regional human rights instruments,[52] which leads some scholars to conclude

---

[46] *E.g.* CRC Committee, *Concluding Observations: Azerbaijan* (UN Doc. CRC/C/66, 1997), para. 306; *Mozambique* (UN Doc. CRC/C/114, 2002), para. 306; *El Salvador* (UN Doc. CRC/C/15/Add.232, 2004), para. 58; and *Japan* (UN Doc. CRC/C/15/Add.231, 2004), para. 50.

[47] *E.g.* CRC Committee, *Concluding Observations: India* (UN Doc. CRC/C/94, 2000), para. 90.

[48] *E.g.* CRC Committee, *Concluding Observations: Gabon* (UN Doc. CRC/C/114, 2002), para. 230; *Nigeria* (UN Doc. CRC/C/50, 1996), para. 91; *Burkina Faso* (UN Doc. CRC/C/121, 2002), para. 478; and *Madagascar* (UN Doc. CRC/C/133, 2004), para. 309.

[49] M. Nowak, 'The right to education—Its meaning, significance and limitations', *Netherlands Quarterly of Human Rights* 4, 1991, p. 423.

[50] Van Bueren subscribes to the viewpoint that the international obligation to establish a system of education and make it accessible to all on the basis of equal opportunities, is traditionally limited to the more formal or professional types of instruction given in institutions (G. Van Bueren, *The International Law on the Rights of the Child, o.c.* (note 18), p. 233).

[51] *Travaux Préparatoires* (UN Docs. E/CN.4/1989/WG.1/CRP.1, 1989, p. 33; E/CN.4/1989/48, 1989, para. 458); See also the statement of Japan contra the inclusion of pre-primary education (UN Doc. E/CN.4/1989/48, 1989), para. 722.

[52] Some non-binding standards, on the contrary, advocate for the introduction and improvement of early child-hood education: see for instance Article 5 of the World Declaration on Education for All, adopted in 1990 in Jomtien (Thailand), *o.c.* (note 42), p. 76; and in Article 7(i) of the Dakar Framework for Action, adopted in 2000 in Dakar (Senegal), in: *o.c.* (note 42),

that there exists no such obligation.[53] The practice of the CRC Committee however points to the inclusion of pre-schooling. The Committee indeed asks the States in its reporting guidelines to report on 'any system or extensive initiatives by the State to provide early development and education services for young children'.[54] Also during the reporting procedure States are congratulated for having a network of pre-school facilities[55] and encouraged to set up or expand (State-run) pre-school establishments[56] as well as to raise awareness of the importance of early childhood education,[57] to increase enrolment at the pre-school level,[58] and to increase the resources devoted to early childhood development.[59] Following a day of general discussion on 'implementing child rights in early childhood', the Committee further recommended that States Parties consider making early childhood education an integral part of basic/primary education.[60]

The Convention is furthermore equally silent about the length of primary, secondary and higher education and also in Committee practice no definition in terms of age can be found. This aspect is hence left to the discretion of the States Parties. Only with regard to the duration of compulsory education—in practice often covering primary education and partly

p. 8. A strong plea for an important role of governments in early childhood education can also be found in K. Annan, *We the Children, Meeting the promises of the World Summit for Children* (New York, UNICEF, 2001), pp. 63–65 and p. 71.

[53] G. Van Bueren, *The International Law on the Rights of the Child, o.c.* (note 18), p. 234 and K. Tomaševski, *Education Denied* (London/New York, Zed Books, 2003), p. 53.

[54] CRC Committee, *General Guidelines regarding the form and the contents of the periodic reports* (UN Doc. CRC/C/58, 1996), para. 106.

[55] *E.g.* CRC Committee, *Concluding Observations: Portugal* (UN Doc. CRC/C/46, 1995), para. 149.

[56] *E.g.* CRC Committee, *Concluding Observations: Sri Lanka* (UN Doc. CRC/C/43, 1995), paras. 154 and 173; *Tajikistan* (UN Doc. CRC/C/100, 2000), para. 310; *Mauritania* (UN Doc. CRC/C/111, 2001), para. 73; *Turkey* (UN Doc. CRC/C/108, 2001), para. 136; *Lesotho* (UN Doc. CRC/C/103, 2001), paras. 361–362; *Georgia* (UN Doc. CRC/C/97, 2000), paras. 128–129; *Kyrgyzstan* (UN Doc. CRC/C/97, 2000), paras. 318–319; *St. Vincent and the Grenadines* (UN Doc. CRC/C/118, 2002), para. 454; *Portugal* (UN Doc. CRC/C/111, 2001), paras. 246–247; *Sweden* (UN Doc. CRC/C/84, 1999), para. 147; *India* (Doc. CRC/C/15/Add.228, 2004), para. 65; *Indonesia* (UN Doc. CRC/C/15/Add.223, 2004), para. 63; and *El Salvador* (UN Doc. CRC/C/15/Add.232, 2004), para. 58.

[57] *E.g.* CRC Committee, *Concluding Observations: Tajikistan* (UN Doc. CRC/C/100, 2000), para. 310; *Niger* (UN Doc. CRC/C/118, 2002), para. 184; *Tunisia* (UN Doc. CRC/C/118, 2002), para. 296; and *India* (UN Doc. CRC/C/15.Add.228, 2004), para. 65.

[58] *E.g.* CRC Committee, *Concluding Observations: Ukraine* (UN Doc. CRC/C/121, 2002), para. 354; and *Madagascar* (UN Doc. CRC/C/133, 2004), para. 309.

[59] *E.g.* CRC Committee, *Concluding Observations: the Libyan Arab Jamahiriya* (UN Doc. CRC/C/132, 2003), para. 385.

[60] CRC Committee, *Day of General Discussion on Implementing child rights in early childhood* (UN Doc. CRC/C/143, 2005), para. 553. See also: UN Doc. CRC/C/137, 2004, paras. 8–9.

secondary education—, the CRC Committee gave some indications. It stated that governments should establish a minimum and maximum age for the completion of compulsory education[61] and put forward that the end of compulsory education should coincide with the minimum age for employment.[62] This is elaborated upon under No. 17.

1.1.2 *Available and Accessible Education*[63]

11. Article 28(1) imposes an obligation on the States to achieve the right to education by making it 'available' and 'accessible' at the level of primary, secondary and higher education. Looking at the text of Article 28, one notices that only in relation to secondary education both terms are explicitly mentioned. As regards primary education, only the availability aspect is mentioned whilst for higher education, only the accessibility aspect is referred to. Still, it is acceptable that both the availability aspect and the accessibility aspect are relevant to all levels of education since both aspects are interlinked. Making education accessible implies in the first place that education should be made available; making education available would have no sense if it would not be accessible. The degree of accessibility may however differ according to the level of education, as will be pointed out below.

12. In the first place, the States Parties under the CRC should make education *available*. This embodies the obligation to take financial and technical actions in order to ensure that an education system of good quality is established

---

[61] *E.g.* CRC Committee, *Concluding Observations: Congo* (UN Doc. CRC/C/108, 2001), para. 210.

[62] *E.g.* CRC Committee, *Concluding Observations: Nicaragua* (UN Doc. CRC/C/43, 1995), para. 65; *Ukraine* (UN Doc. CRC/C/46, 1995), paras. 54 and 63; *Tunisia* (UN Doc. CRC/C/43, 1995), para. 125; *Senegal* (UN Doc. CRC/C/46, 1995), paras. 125 and 139; *Korea* (UN Doc. UN Doc. CRC/C/50, 1996), paras. 166 and 171; and *Niger* (UN Doc. CRC/C/118, 2002), paras. 148–149.

[63] These are two components of the four 'A' scheme, put forward by the CESCR Committee in its analysis of the content of the right to receive education. The other two components, being the 'acceptability' and the 'adaptability' of education are discussed further in this text under No. 19, 34, 35 *et seq.*, and 46 *et seq.* (The four 'A' scheme can be found in: CESCR Committee, *General Comment No. 13 on the Right to Education* (UN Doc. E/C.12/1999/10, 1999), para. 6 and in the findings of the Special Rapporteur on the right to education: K. Tomaševski, *Preliminary report of the Special Rapporteur on the right to education* (UN Doc. E/CN.4/1999/49, 1998), Chapter II, paras. 51–74; K. Tomaševski, *Progress Report of the Special Rapporteur on the Right to Education 1999/25* (UN Doc. E/CN.4/2000/6, 2000), paras. 32–65; K. Tomaševski, *Annual Report of the Special Rapporteur on the Right to Education 2001/29* (UN Doc. E/CN.4/2002/60, 2002), table on p. 13; K. Tomaševski, *Right to Education Primer 3: Human rights obligations: making education available, accessible, acceptable and adaptable*, o.c. (note 3), p. 14; and K. Tomaševski, *Education Denied*, o.c. (note 53), pp. 51–52.

and maintained. The kind of facilities the State has to ensure for a good functioning of its educational system depends upon among others the developmental context within that State. The question as to when exactly the obligation to make education available is fulfilled, can therefore only be answered on a case-by-case basis.[64] Some facilities are indispensable in all countries, regardless of their developmental status. This is the case for a good infrastructure, including buildings, sanitation facilities for both sexes and safe drinking water as well as practical and didactical equipment.[65] The CRC Committee often expressed its concern in this regard when studying the reports of the developing countries.[66] Also competent teachers should be sufficiently present in all countries. The Special Rapporteur on the right to education points at the fact that teachers should be educated and trained to teach and should have perfect knowledge of the language in which they teach.[67] This concern is shared by the CRC Committee, which often recommends the training of teachers in its concluding observations[68] and also points at the importance of the ability of teachers to speak in local languages.[69] Also the training and recruitment of more female teachers is recommended.[70] All these factors (the efforts and quality of the teachers, the availability and quality of the teaching materials, etc.) are determinant for a minimum quality of education, which should be attained and maintained in all countries regardless their economic situation. Other facilities, such as a library, computer services and information technology, will only be feasible in developed countries.[71] The recommendations of the CRC Committee therefore clearly differ according to the developmental context of a State.

---

[64] CESCR Committee, *General Comment No. 13 on the Right to Education* (UN Doc. E/C.12/1999/10, 1999), para. 6.

[65] *Ibid.*, para. 6.

[66] *E.g.* CRC Committee, *Concluding Observations: India* (UN Doc. CRC/C/94, 2000), para. 88; *The Gambia* (UN Doc. CRC/C/111, 2001), para. 452; *The Democratic Republic of the Congo* (UN Doc. CRC/C/108, 2001), para. 210; *Jamaica* (UN Doc. CRC/C/38, 1995), para. 153; and *Paraguay* (UN Doc. CRC/C/111, 2001), paras. 512–513.

[67] K. Tomaševski, *Right to Education Primer 3: Human rights obligations: making education available, accessible, acceptable and adaptable, o.c.* (note 3), p. 24.

[68] *E.g.* CRC Committee, *Concluding Observations: Namibia* (UN Doc. CRC/C/24, 1994), para. 62; *Honduras* (UN Doc. CRC/C/34, 1994), para. 57, *Guinea-Bissau* (UN Doc. CRC/C/118, 2002), para. 75; and *Niger* (UN Doc. CRC/C/118, 2002), para. 184.

[69] *E.g.* CRC Committee, *Concluding Observations: Greece* (UN Doc. CRC/C/114, 2002), para. 159; and *Sudan* (UN Doc. CRC/C/121, 2002), para. 275.

[70] *E.g.* CRC Committee, *Concluding Observations: Mozambique* (UN Doc. CRC/C/114, 2002), para. 306; *Burkina Faso* (UN Doc. CRC/C/121, 2002), para. 478; and *New Zealand* (UN Doc. CRC/C/133, 2004), para. 309.

[71] CESCR Committee, *General Comment No. 13 on the Right to Education* (UN Doc. E/C.12/1999/10, 1999), para. 6.

Some countries will be encouraged by the Committee to increase the computerization of schools,[72] whilst the Committee is silent about these expensive facilities in its recommendations to other countries.

The availability obligation can be fulfilled by means of several models. Firstly, the government can establish a network of public schools. Secondly, the government can fund institutions run by non-state actors. And thirdly, the government can have a mixture of both public schools and (funded) private schools. Most countries have the latter model.[73] If a government chooses for one of the last two models, it has the obligation to protect the enjoyment of the right to education in all its aspects, such as free and compulsory primary education and equal access to education by means of for instance legislative measures, state supervision and subsidies.[74]

13. In the second place, States should guarantee *access* to education. According to the CESCR Committee, the accessibility aspect has three overlapping dimensions.[75]

Firstly, the educational institutions and programmes should be accessible to all children, without discrimination on any of the prohibited grounds. Special attention must be paid to the most vulnerable groups in society.[76] At the level of primary and secondary education, the words 'all' and 'every child' in Article 28(1) confirm general accessibility of educational institutions and forms of education. At these levels no distinction may be made on the basis of the child's apparent capacity or ability. As regards higher education, on the contrary, States have the possibility to make access to higher education dependent on the capacities of the students. 'Capacity' may be understood as the ability to absorb the education.[77] Usually the 'capacity' is validated by submission of the necessary diplomas and/or participation to entrance examinations. The CESCR Committee, however, points at the fact that the capacity of individuals should be assessed by reference

[72] *E.g.* CRC Committee, *Concluding Observations: St. Vincent and the Grenadines* (UN Doc. CRC/C/118, 2002), para. 454; and Portugal (UN Doc. CRC/C/111, 2001), para. 247.

[73] K. Tomaševski, *Right to Education Primer 3: Human rights obligations: making education available, accessible, acceptable and adaptable, o.c.* (note 3), pp. 13 and 19–20.

[74] M. Nowak, 'The Right to Education', *l.c.* (note 3), pp. 257–258.

[75] CESCR Committee, *General Comment No. 13 on the Right to Education* (UN Doc. E/C.12/1999/10, 1999), para. 6.

[76] *Cf. infra* No. 34.

[77] *Cf.* Arajärvi's statement with regard to the word 'merit' in Article 26 of the UDHR: P. Arajärvi, 'Article 26', in: G. Alfredsson and A. Eide (eds.), *The Universal Declaration of Human Rights: A Common Standard of Achievement* (The Hague, Martinus Nijhoff Publishers, 1999), p. 555.

to all their relevant expertise and experience.[78] One should thus not solely focus on success in examinations, but also have regard to more practical capacities.[79] As 'capacity' consists in a sense of teachable skills, which depend greatly on the opportunities a child gets in life, the CRC Committee emphasises the importance of equal opportunities in higher education. This is reflected in its detailed reporting requirements, which ask the States Parties to indicate the rate of access to higher education by age, gender and national, social and ethnic origin.[80] According to Hodgkin and Newell this reporting requirement reveals a minimum obligation for the States Parties to introduce supporting measures, such as financial assistance enabling poor children to take entrance examinations to higher education courses and to award scholarships if they succeed.[81] Whether—next to the capacity of the child—other differences in treatment as to inscription are allowed under Article 28(1) remains an open question. The wording of Article 28(1) is not sufficiently clear in this sense nor is the practice of the CRC Committee. The regulation of access to education with regard to other grounds of refusal to register, such as the failure to reach the deadline of inscription or bad behaviour of the pupil in the past, can therefore be considered as left to the States Parties' discretion.

Secondly, the concept refers to the physical accessibility of education: education has to be provided within a reasonable and safe distance. Either a child should be able to attend education at some reasonably convenient geographic location (*e.g.* a neighbouring school) or he or she should have access to education via modern technology (*e.g.* a distance learning programme).[82] The CRC Committee often recommends States to ensure that children in rural areas have access to education.[83] Hereto, special measures

[78] CESCR Committee, *General Comment No. 13 on the Right to Education* (UN Doc. E/C.12/1999/10, 1999), para. 19.

[79] R. Hodgkin and P. Newell, *Implementation Handbook for the Convention on the Rights of the Child* (New York/Genève, UNICEF, 2002), p. 420.

[80] CRC Committee, *General Guidelines regarding the form and the contents of the periodic reports* (UN Doc. CRC/C/58, 1996), para. 107.

[81] R. Hodgkin and P. Newell, *o.c.* (note 79), p. 420.

[82] CESCR Committee, *General Comment No. 13 on the Right to Education* (UN Doc. E/C.12/1999/10, 1999), para. 6.

[83] *E.g.* the CRC Committee, *Concluding Observations: Jordan* (UN Doc. CRC/C/29, 1994), para. 131; *Colombia* (UN Doc. CRC/C/38, 1995), para. 96; *Yemen* (UN Doc. CRC/C/50, 1996), paras. 63 and 71; *Lesotho* (UN Doc. CRC/C/103, 2001), paras. 361–362; *Georgia* (UN Doc. CRC/C/97, 2000), para. 128; *Sierra Leone* (UN Doc. CRC/C/94, 2000), paras. 180–181; *Mexico* (UN Doc. CRC/C/90, 1999), para. 187; and *Poland* (UN Doc. CRC/C/121, 2002), para. 538.

are required, such as the facilitation of transport and the construction of additional schools in isolated areas.[84]

Thirdly, there is the economic accessibility, *i.e.* education must be affordable to all. This implies positive obligations, such as making access to education free of charges and introducing scholarships.[85] These obligations differ, however, according to the level of education. As will become clear below, Article 28(1) requires that primary education is free of charges but in principle implicitly endorses the charging of fees in secondary and higher education. Charging fees for post-primary education, however, has the unfortunate side-effect that education becomes unaffordable and thus inaccessible to a lot of children.[86] In most cases States therefore will have to refrain from charging fees and even provide some kind of financial support in order to comply with the progressive realisation of the accessibility of secondary and higher education.

1.1.3 *Free Education*

14. At the level of primary education, the CRC requires that education is 'free'. This obligation is in line with traditional human rights law on primary education.[87] The cost-free aspect of primary education nevertheless was a point of discussion during the drafting of the Convention. Several States Parties attempted to reduce the protection of this right, as guaranteed in the CESCR. Proposals were made to only impose an obligation to organise cost-free primary education 'as early as the circumstances permit',[88] 'as early as permitted by national resources available'[89] or 'as early as possible'.[90] These restrictions were omitted, thanks to the protest by other

---

[84] *E.g.* CRC Committee, *Concluding Observations: the Democratic Republic of the Congo* (UN Doc. CRC/C/108, 2001), para. 210; and *Mozambique* (UN Doc. CRC/C/114, 2002), para. 306.

[85] CESCR Committee, *General Comment No. 13 on the Right to Education* (UN Doc. E/C.12/1999/10, 1999), para. 6.

[86] K. Tomaševski, *Right to Education Primer 3: Human rights obligations: making education available, accessible, acceptable and adaptable*, *o.c.* (note 3), p. 14.

[87] *Cf.* also Article 26(1) of the UDHR, Articles 13(2)(a) and 14 of the CESCR, Article 13(3)(a) of the Protocol of San Salvador to the American Convention on Human Rights in the Area of Economic, Social and Cultural Rights and Article 11(3)(a) of the African Charter on the Rights and Welfare of the Child.

[88] *Travaux Préparatoires* (UN Doc. E/CN.4/1985/64, 1985), para. 58; reproduced in S. Detrick (ed.), *The United Nations Convention on the Rights of the Child: A Guide to the "Travaux Préparatoires"* (Dordrecht, Boston, London, Martinus Nijhoff Publishers, 1992), p. 384.

[89] *Travaux Préparatoires* (UN Doc. E/CN.4/1985/64, 1985), para. 63; reproduced in S. Detrick (ed.), *The United Nations Convention on the Rights of the Child: A Guide to the "Travaux Préparatoires"*, *o.c.* (note 88), p. 385.

[90] *Travaux Préparatoires* (UN Doc. E/CN.4/1985/64, 1985), para. 66; reproduced in S. Detrick

States.[91] States Parties to the CRC, hence, must take immediate steps in order to make primary education cost-free. This should be done for 'all', meaning every child and not just low-income children or other categories.[92] The CESCR Committee clarified in its General Comment No. 11 that cost-free education does not only mean that access to education should be free of charge and the government thus should abstain from imposing registration fees. Also all other direct and indirect costs, such as compulsory levies on parents (sometimes portrayed as being voluntary, when in fact they are not), or the obligation to wear a relatively expensive school uniform, should be eliminated.[93] Coomans adds to this list expenses for textbooks and supplies, the costs of extra lessons, expenses for meals and school canteens, school transport, and medical expenses.[94] The CRC Committee considers the cost-free aspect of primary education as crucial and therefore strongly recommends the States to fulfil this obligation.[95] It follows the view of the CESCR Committee in the sense that the notion 'free' goes beyond the principle of free access. In its concluding observations to the States Parties' reports, the CRC Committee points out that the obligation to provide for cost-free primary education also entails an obligation of assistance to purchase uniforms and school books, at least for children of poor families.[96] It is worth mentioning that international human rights law does not exempt the parents and the broader community of bearing the costs of education in general. Parents and the community may finance children's education through gen-

(ed.), *The United Nations Convention on the Rights of the Child: A Guide to the "Travaux Préparatoires"*, *o.c.* (note 88), p. 385 and *Travaux Préparatoires* (E/CN.4/1988/WG.1/WP.1/Rev.1.)

[91] *Travaux Préparatoires* (UN Docs. E/CN.4/1985/64, 1985, paras. 60 and 67; E/CN.4/1989/48, 1989, paras. 461–462); reproduced in S. Detrick (ed.), *The United Nations Convention on the Rights of the Child: A Guide to the "Travaux Préparatoires"*, *o.c.* (note 88), pp. 384–385 and p. 392.

[92] Three States entered reservations to this subparagraph: Samoa, Singapore and Swaziland. See R. Hodgkin and P. Newell, *o.c.* (note 79), p. 416.

[93] CESCR Committee, *General Comment No. 11 on plans of action for primary education* (UN Doc. E/C.12/1999/4, 1999), para. 7.

[94] F. Coomans, 'In search of the core content of the right to education', *l.c.* (note 3), p. 228.

[95] *E.g.* CRC Committee, *Concluding Observations: Senegal* (UN Doc. CRC/C/46, 1995), paras. 128 and 142; *Lebanon* (UN Doc. CRC/C/54, 1996), para. 56; *Zimbabwe* (UN Doc. CRC/C/54, 1996), para. 89; *Kenya* (UN Doc. CRC/C/111, 2001), para. 135; *Cameroon* (UN Doc. CRC/C/111, 2001), paras. 379–380; the Ivory Coast (UN Doc. CRC/C/108, 2001), paras. 337–338; *the Gambia* (UN Doc. CRC/C/111, 2001), paras. 452–453; and *South Africa* (UN Doc. CRC/C/94, 2000), para. 447.

[96] *E.g.* CRC Committee, *Concluding Observations: Sierra Leone* (UN Doc. CRC/C/94, 2000), paras. 180–181; *the Central African Republic* (UN Doc. CRC/C/100, 2000), para. 468; *Cameroon* (UN Doc. CRC/C/111, 2001), para. 380; *Guinea-Bissau* (UN Doc. CRC/C/118, 2002), para. 75; and *Mozambique* (UN Doc. CRC/C/114, 2002), para. 306.

eral taxation. It is then the obligation of the State to prioritise primary education in resource allocation.[97]

As has already been pointed out above (*cf. supra* No. 7), the obligation under Article 28(1)(a) to ensure free education is not as strong as the obligation under Article 13(2)(a) of the CESCR. Firstly, States Parties to the CRC must only fulfil this obligation in a progressive manner, and not immediately, as the CESCR requires. Secondly, States Parties to the CRC have no obligation of conduct to draw up a national action plan for progressively implementing the right to free primary education, as is required under Article 14 of the CESCR. The CRC Committee, however, recommended the elaboration of such an 'action plan' or 'detailed study' on a number of occasions.[98]

15. At the level of secondary education, the States should fulfil their obligation to develop different forms of secondary education by taking 'appropriate measures such as the introduction of *free* education and offering *financial assistance* in case of need'. The introduction of cost-free secondary education is thus much more cautiously formulated than at the level of primary education. This cautious formulation is in line with the existing standards on secondary education[99] and reflects the recognition that its realisation is at the present beyond the resources of numerous countries.[100] The drafters of the CRC, however, opted for a formulation, which offers a weaker protection than the CESCR (*cf. supra* No. 7). The term '*such as*' indeed reflects a weaker protection than the phrase '*in particular*' in Article 13(2)(b) of the CESCR.[101] Although States Parties to the CESCR should give priority to make

[97] K. Tomaševski, *Preliminary report of the Special Rapporteur on the right to education*, (UN Doc. E/CN.4/1999/49, 1998), para. 35; K. Tomaševski, *Progress Report of the Special Rapporteur on the Right to Education 1999/25*, (UN Doc. E/CN.4/2000/6, 2000), paras. 49–50; and K. Tomaševski, *Right to Education Primer 2: Free and compulsory education for all children: the gap between promise and performance* (Lund, Raoul Wallenberg Institute, 2001), p. 20.

[98] *E.g.* CRC Committee, *Concluding Observations*: *Vanuatu* (UN Doc. CRC/C/15/Add.111, 1999), para. 21; and *Mauritius* (UN Doc. CRC/C/15/Add.64, 1996), para 29.

[99] The introduction of cost-free secondary education is also cautiously formulated in other human rights instruments: See Article 26 of the UDHR, which states that education should be free 'at least' in the elementary and fundamental stages; Article 13(2)(b) of the CESCR and Article 13(3)(b) of the Protocol of San Salvador to the American Convention on Human Rights in the Area of Economic, Social and Cultural Rights, which state that secondary education should be made available and accessible to all by every appropriate means and 'in particular' by the progressive introduction of free education. Article 11(3)(a) of the African Charter on the Rights and Welfare of the Child holds the strongest formulation by stating that the States Parties shall progressively make secondary education free and accessible to all.

[100] R. Hodgkin and P. Newell, *o.c.* (note 79), p. 417.

[101] S. Detrick, *A Commentary on the United Nations Convention on the Rights of the Child* (The

primary education free of charge, they have a clear obligation to take steps towards the realisation of cost-free secondary education.[102] The CRC, on the other hand, refers to the introduction of cost-free secondary education merely as an example of how education could be made accessible to all children. One may assume that States could also fulfil this obligation by taking other appropriate measures.[103] Although cost-free secondary education is no compulsory measure, its importance and efficiency has been emphasised. In this sense the CRC Committee expressed its concern about the parental costs in secondary education.[104] Also the Special Rapporteur on the right to education and some scholars stress that the introduction of cost-free education constitutes the most efficient way for States to fulfil their obligations regarding secondary education.[105]

16. At the level of higher education, States Parties have even more limited obligations regarding the cost-free aspect than at the level of secondary education. Article 28(1) does not oblige governments to organise free higher education nor to take some steps in this direction. The *Travaux Préparatoires* nevertheless reveal that the phrase 'in particular by the progressive introduction of free education', enshrined in Article 13(2)(c) of the CESCR was included in one of the draft texts of the CRC.[106] The opposition of some more wealthy countries, such as the Netherlands, Great-Britain, Finland and Japan eventually resulted in the omission of this phrase.[107] The obligations under the CRC are hence less strong than the ones under the equivalent article in

---

Hague/Boston/Londen, Martinus Nijhoff Publishers, 1999), p. 481 and D. Hodgson, *l.c.* (note 18), pp. 246–247.

[102] CESCR Committee, *General Comment No. 13 on the Right to Education* (UN Doc. E/C.12/1999/10, 1999), para. 14.

[103] *Travaux Préparatoires* (UN Doc. E/CN.4/1989/48, 1989), para. 464; reproduced in S. Detrick (ed.), *The United Nations Convention on the Rights of the Child: A Guide to the "Travaux Préparatoires"*, *o.c.* (note 88), p. 393: 'The representative of Japan indicated that he interpreted the reference in the subparagraph to free education as merely giving an example of how education could be made accessible to all children, and not to mean that free education was a measure which States Parties were obliged to adopt'.

[104] *E.g.* CRC Committee, *Concluding Observations: Zimbabwe* (UN Doc. CRC/C/54, 1996), para. 89; and *Barbados* (UN Doc. CRC/C/87, 1999), para. 57.

[105] K. Tomaševski, *Right to Education Primer 3: Human rights obligations: making education available, accessible, acceptable and adaptable*, *o.c.* (note 3), p. 14. See also G. Van Bueren, *The International Law on the Rights of the Child*, *o.c.* (note 18), p. 236.

[106] *Travaux Préparatoires* (UN Doc. E/CN.4/1989/48, 1989), para. 459; reproduced in S. Detrick, *The United Nations Convention on the Rights of the Child: A Guide to the "Travaux Préparatoires"*, *o.c.* (note 88), p. 391.

[107] *Travaux Préparatoires* (UN Doc. E/CN.4/1989/48, 1989), paras. 465–466; reproduced in S. Detrick, *The United Nations Convention on the Rights of the Child: A Guide to the "Travaux Préparatoires"*, *o.c.* (note 88), p. 393.

the CESCR, which imposes an obligation on States Parties to take steps in order to make higher education free of charge.[108] It is worth mentioning that there is a current global priority for primary education, which has focused attention away from secondary and tertiary education.[109] The CRC reinforces this trend by decreasing the protection on those levels. This is however tempered by the emphasis of the CRC Committee on the importance of equal access and opportunities in higher education,[110] which, in the opinion of Hodgkin and Newell, reveals a minimum obligation for States Parties to introduce supporting measures, such as financial assistance enabling poor children to take entrance examinations to higher education courses and to award scholarships if they succeed.[111]

1.1.4 *Compulsory Education*

17. At the level of primary education, the States Parties are not only obliged to make primary education free, they also should make it compulsory. The principle of compulsory education is shared by several human rights treaties[112] and is based on the belief that, in the best interest of the child, education cannot be refused below a certain level. It ensures that the child's right to receive education shall not be impeded by for instance parental neglect, abuse or ignorance, cultural resistance or child labour.[113] The word 'compulsory' should thus be interpreted as protecting the child's rights and not in a sense that it implies coercion by the State or the family to follow a specific type of education nor in the sense that the State has a monopoly over education.[114] The principles of free education and compulsory education are interrelated. By placing a duty on the government to provide free

---

[108] S. Detrick, *A Commentary on the United Nations Convention on the Rights of the Child*, *o.c.* (note 101), p. 483 and D. Hodgson, *l.c.* (note 18), p. 245.

[109] K. Tomaševski, *Right to Education Primer 3: Human rights obligations: making education available, accessible, acceptable and adaptable*, *o.c.* (note 3), p. 17.

[110] CRC Committee, *General Guidelines regarding the form and the contents of the periodic reports* (UN Doc. CRC/C/58, 1996), para. 107.

[111] R. Hodgkin and P. Newell, *o.c.* (note 79), p. 420.

[112] See also Article 26(1) of the UDHR; Article 13(2)(a) and 14 of the CESCR; Article 13(3)(a) of the Protocol of San Salvador to the American Convention on Human Rights in the Area of Economic, Social and Cultural Rights and Article 11(3)(a) of the African Charter on the Rights and Welfare of the Child.

[113] CESCR Committee, *General Comment No. 11 on plans of action for primary education* (UN Doc. E/C.12/1999/4, 1999), para. 6. See also M. Mehedi, *o.c.* (note 2), paras. 39 and 59 and D. Hodgson, *l.c.* (note 18), p. 241.

[114] K. Halvorsen, 'Notes on the Realization of the Human Right to Education', *Human Rights Quarterly* 12, 1990, pp. 351–352.

education, attendance can be made compulsory by law.[115] The CRC Committee puts therefore, often in connection with the cost-free aspect, much weight to the fact that primary education has to be made compulsory.[116]

Compulsory education implies some positive obligations for the States. Firstly, they should take legislative measures, imposing compulsory education to a certain minimum age. Secondly,—as pointed out by several commentators—the States should—next to abolishing registration fees in primary education—adopt alternative strategies, aimed at promoting school attendance, such as transport facilities and nutritional provision.[117] A similar policy is promoted by the CRC Committee, which recommends the provision of meals and health counselling services[118] as well as free transportation for disadvantaged children in its concluding observations to the States Parties reports.[119] Also with regard to working children, the Committee made some suggestions in order to ensure their education rights. This is elaborated upon below under No. 26 and 34. It should be stressed that, as is the case for the obligation to make primary education free, the obligation to make primary education compulsory under Article 28(1)(a) is not as strong as the one under 13(2)(a) of the CESCR. Compulsory primary education should only be realised progressively, and without the drafting of a detailed action plan. (*cf. supra* No. 7 and 14).

Making education compulsory does not mean making school attendance compulsory. Education and school are not synonymous. As Hodgkin and Newell rightly point out, children can be educated outside schools, though it is unusual, and, attendance at school does not necessarily mean that the child is being educated.[120] Article 28(1)(e) of the CRC, imposing an obligation on the States Parties to increase school attendance reflects however the underlying believe of the drafters that schools in general are the best places for children to receive education (*cf. infra* No. 25–27).[121]

---

[115] G. Van Bueren, *The International Law on the Rights of the Child, o.c.* (note 18), p. 238.

[116] *E.g.* CRC Committee, *Concluding Observations: Senegal* (UN Doc. CRC/C/46, 1995), paras. 128 and 142; *Zimbabwe* (UN Doc. CRC/C/54, 1996), para. 89; *Nepal* (UN Doc. CRC/C/54, 1996), para. 167; *Cambodia* (UN Doc. CRC/C/97, 2000), paras. 384–385; *Oman* (UN Doc. CRC/C/111, 2001), paras. 191–192; *the Ivory Coast* (UN Doc. CRC/C/108, 2001), paras. 337–338; *the Maldives* (UN Doc. CRC/C/79, 1998), para. 236; and *Bhutan* (UN Doc. CRC/C/108, 2001), paras. 470–471.

[117] M. Mehedi, *o.c.* (note 2), para. 55 and G. Van Bueren, *The International Law on the Rights of the Child, o.c.* (note 18), pp. 238–239.

[118] *E.g.* CRC Committee, *Concluding Observations: Honduras* (UN Doc. CRC/C/34, 1994), para. 58; and *Grenada* (UN Doc. CRC/C/94, 2000), para. 408.

[119] *E.g.* CRC Committee, *Concluding Observations: Mozambique* (UN Doc. CRC/C/114, 2002), para. 306.

[120] R. Hodgkin and P. Newell, *o.c.* (note 79), p. 417.

[121] This is confirmed by some scholars. *E.g.* Wilson states that 'compulsory schooling can

On the kind of skills the child should have acquired before leaving compulsory education, the CRC as well as the Committee are completely silent. This may be considered as left to the States Parties' discretion.

The Convention is also silent about the duration of compulsory education. In its concluding observations to the States Parties' reports, the CRC Committee gives some indications regarding the end of compulsory education. The Committee is of the opinion that the end of compulsory education should coincide with the minimum age for employment.[122] The CRC itself does not determine a minimum age for admissions to employment but merely imposes an obligation on the States to provide for a minimum age.[123] Under Article 2(3) of the ILO-Convention No. 138 there is an international obligation not to establish this minimum under the age of completion of compulsory schooling and, in any case, not under the age of 15.[124] According to the nature or the circumstances in which the work is carried out, this Convention also imposes other age limits (14, 16, and 18). Often, the age-limit of 15 is recommended by the CRC Committee.[125] In other cases, the Committee recommended rather the age limit of 14 or 16.[126] In yet other cases, the Committee merely recommended the States to clearly set an age for admission to and completion of compulsory education,[127] or else simply

be the key to combat the effects of private discrimination, which may impact on the education of girls.': D. Wilson, 'Human Rights: Promoting Gender Equality in and through education', *PROSPECTS, UNESCO journal on comparative education* 34, No. 1, 2004, p. 11.

[122] *E.g.* CRC Committee, *Concluding Observations: Nicaragua* (UN Doc. CRC/C/43, 1995), para. 65; *Ukraine* (UN Doc. CRC/C/46, 1995), paras. 54 and 63; *Tunisia* (UN Doc. CRC/C/43, 1995), para. 125; *Senegal* (UN Doc. CRC/C/46, 1995), paras. 125 and 139; *Korea* (UN Doc. CRC/C/50, 1996), paras. 166 and 171; and *Niger* (UN Doc. CRC/C/118, 2002), paras. 148–149.

[123] Article 32 of the CRC merely states that child labour may not interfere with the child's education. A similar provision is entrenched in Article 7(3) of the Revised European Social Charter (1996).

[124] ILO-Convention No. 138, Convention concerning Minimum Age for Admission to Employment, adopted on 26 June 1973, entered into force 19 June 1976.

[125] *E.g.* CRC Committee, *Concluding Observations: Sri Lanka* (UN Doc. CRC/C/43, 1995), para. 175 and *Zimbabwe* (UN Doc. CRC/C/54, 1996), para. 102.

[126] See for instance the concluding observations of the CRC Committee to the initial report of St. Vincent and the Grenadines in which the Committee recommended that the Government raise the age of compulsory education from 14 to 16 (UN Doc. CRC/C/118, 2002), para. 454; the concluding observations to the initial report of Burundi in which the Committee recommended to raise the school-leaving age to 16 (UN Doc. CRC/C/100, 2000), para. 110; the concluding observations to the initial report of Mauritania in which the Committee recommended that compulsory education should last from the age of 6 until the age of 14 (UN Doc. CRC/C/111, 2001), para. 73.

[127] *E.g.* CRC Committee, *Concluding Observations: the Democratic Republic of the Congo* (UN Doc. CRC/C/108, 2001), para. 210; *Cameroon* (UN Doc. CRC/C/111, 2001), para. 349; *the Solomon Islands* (UN Doc. CRC/C/132, 2003), para. 303; and *Pakistan* (UN Doc. CRC/C/133, 2004), para. 194.

put forward a number of years instead of recommending age limits.[128] Usually, compulsory education lasts from six till 15 years,[129] which in the majority of the countries partly envelops secondary education.[130]

The above listed obligations are duties of the government. It should however be mentioned that the principle of compulsory education implies one of the few obligations in international human rights law imposed upon the individual (the child) itself, in the form of an implied obligation to exercise its right to education.[131]

18. As far as secondary and higher education are concerned, Article 28(1) does not impose a duty on the States to make either compulsory. It should nevertheless be mentioned that although no notion is made in Article 28(1)(b) of compulsory secondary education, in many countries compulsory education has been lengthened far beyond primary education.[132]

1.1.5 *Content of Education*

19. Article 28(1) does not spell out the content of the curriculum at primary, secondary and higher level. This is mainly left to the discretion of the States Parties. States should, however, make sure that the curriculum at all levels of education is 'acceptable' to the child, which means that the substance of education should among others things be relevant, culturally appropriate and of good quality.[133] The State may impose minimum educational standards to private educational institutions to make sure that the acceptability criterion is reached.[134] This criterion is further subject to the objectives as enumerated in Article 29(1) of the CRC. The curriculum should be composed in such a way that the education offered a) enables a child to freely develop his or her personality, talents, mental and physical abilities;

---

[128] In its concluding observations to the initial report of Nicaragua for instance, the Committee put forward that compulsory education should take nine years (UN Doc. CRC/C/43, 1995), para. 65.

[129] K. Tomaševski, *Right to Education Primer 3: Human rights obligations: making education available, accessible, acceptable and adaptable*, o.c. (note 3), p. 10.

[130] K. Tomaševski, *Right to Education Primer 2: Free and compulsory education for all children: the gap between promise and performance*, o.c. (note 97), p. 27. See also A. Melchiorre, *At what age? . . . are school children employed, married and taken into court?* (Lund, Raoul Wallenberg Institute, 2002), 119 p.

[131] P. Arajärvi, 'Article 26', *l.c.* (note 77), p. 554; M. Nowak, 'The Right to Education' *l.c.* (note 3), pp. 253 and 261; and K. Tomaševski, *Preliminary report of the Special Rapporteur on the right to education* (UN Doc. E/CN.4/1999/49, 1998), paras. 75–77.

[132] *Cf. supra* note 130.

[133] CESCR Committee, *General Comment No. 13 on the Right to Education* (UN Doc. E/C.12/1999/10, 1999), para. 6.

[134] Article 29(2) of the CRC.

b) develops respect for human rights, fundamental freedoms and the maintenance of peace; c) develops respect for one's parents, national values of one's country and those of other civilizations; d) enables a child to participate in a free society in the spirit of mutual tolerance and respect for other civilizations, cultures, religions, sexes and e) develops respect for the natural environment. The CRC Committee therefore repeatedly encouraged the States to include education about the CRC—including on the aims enshrined in Art. 29—in the (formal and non-formal)[135] curricula at all levels of schooling.[136] This applies to both State and non-State schools (such as Catholic schools).[137] Emphasis often has been put on teaching about mutual tolerance and respect for other civilizations, cultures and religions[138] as well as teaching about respect for the environment.[139] Also the enclosure of 'education for peace'[140] and of health education, including education on sex, HIV/AIDS, reproductive health and drugs in the school curriculum has often been recommended.[141] Further the Committee has regularly suggested to make the curriculum more relevant to children.[142] Active participation of the pupils in schooling is identified as a strategy to reach this goal.[143] In

[135] *E.g.* CRC Committee, *Concluding Observations: Nicaragua* (UN Doc. CRC/C/43, 1995), paras. 57 and 65.

[136] *E.g.* CRC Committee, *Concluding Observations: Norway* (UN Doc. CRC/C/29, 1994), para. 174; *Colombia* (UN Doc. CRC/C/38, 1995), para. 96; *Denmark* (UN Doc. CRC/C/38, 1995), para. 198; the *United Kingdom of Great-Britain and Northern Ireland* (UN Doc. CRC/C/38, 1995), para. 234; *Canada* (UN Doc. CRC/C/43, 1995), para. 87, *Ukraine* (UN Doc. CRC/C/46, 1995), para. 67; *Belgium* (UN Doc. CRC/C/43, 1995), para. 112, *Germany* (UN Doc. CRC/C/46, 1995), para. 105; *Niger* (UN Doc. CRC/C/118, 2002), para. 147; and *Japan* (UN Doc. CRC/C/15/Add.231, 2004), para. 21.

[137] *E.g.* CRC Committee, *Concluding Observations: the Holy See* (UN Doc. CRC/C/46, 1995), para. 183.

[138] *E.g.* CRC Committee, *Concluding Observations: the Federal Republic of Yugoslavia (Serbia and Montenegro)* (UN Doc. CRC/C/50, 1996), para. 109; *Lebanon* (UN Doc. CRC/C/54, 1996), para. 57; and *Belgium* (UN Doc. CRC/C/118, 2002), para. 117.

[139] *E.g.* CRC Committee, *Concluding Observations: Lebanon* (UN Doc. CRC/C/54, 1996), para. 42.

[140] *E.g.* CRC Committee, *Concluding Observations: Burundi* (UN Doc. CRC/C/100, 2000), para. 151; and *Rwanda* (CRC/C/15/Add.234, para. 57).

[141] *E.g.* CRC Committee, *Concluding Observations: Estonia* (UN Doc. CRC/C/124, 2003), para. 69; *Cyprus* (UN Doc. CRC/C/132, 2003), para. 136; *Argentina* (UN Doc. CRC/C/121, 2002), para. 76; *Indonesia* (UN Doc. CRC/C/Add.223, 2004), para. 59, *New Zealand* (UN Doc. CRC/C/133, 2004), para. 150; *Madagascar* (UN Doc. CRC/C/133, 2004), para. 305; and *Bangladesh* (UN Doc. CRC/C/133, 2004), para. 492. See also CRC Committee, *Day of General Discussion on Children living in a World with AIDS* (UN Doc. CRC/C/79, 1998), Annex VI, para. 243.

[142] *E.g.* CRC Committee, *Concluding Observations: Costa Rica* (UN Doc. UN Doc. CRC/C/94, 2000), para. 233 and *Italy* (UN Doc. CRC/C/15/Add.41, 1995), para. 21.

[143] *E.g.* CRC Committee, *Concluding Observations: Cameroon* (UN Doc. CRC/C/111, 2001) para. 380; *Saudi-Arabia* (UN Doc. CRC/C/103, 2001) para. 414 and *the Netherlands Antilles* (UN Doc. CRC/C/118, 2002), para. 576.

order to make sure that the instruction corresponds to the aims of Article 29, not only the curriculum should be adapted to these aims but also those who are responsible to implement this curriculum. Therefore, the CRC Committee repeatedly recommended that education on the provisions and principles of the Convention should also be included in the training programmes of future teachers[144] and that the teaching methods should be inspired by and reflect the spirit and philosophy of the Convention, in the light of the general principles of the Convention and the provisions of its Article 29.[145] This should also be guaranteed in non-State schools.[146]

In sum, it can be stated that the aims of education laid down in Article 29 put definite limits on types of education, but simultaneously the content of the curriculum stays very general and is left open to many alternatives, which opens the possibility for each culture to determine it in its own way. This offers the possibility to make the substance of education 'adaptable', meaning that it should be flexible so it can adapt to the needs of changing societies and respond to the needs of students within their diverse social and cultural settings.[147] The last aspect calls in other words for 'differentiated education'.[148]

20. The CESCR Committee gives some indications as to the contents of education at each level. As Article 28(1) of the CRC has largely been drawn up among the lines of Article 13(2) of the CESCR, one may suggest that these findings may be read into the text of Article 28(1)(c) of the CRC.

Primary education should, in line with Article 5 of the World Declaration on Education for All, ensure that the basic learning needs of all children are satisfied.[149] Basic learning needs comprise both essential learning tools (such as literacy, oral expression, numeracy, and problem solving) and the

---

[144] *E.g.* CRC Committee, *Concluding Observations: Namibia* (UN Doc. CRC/C/24, 1994), para. 62; *Norway* (UN Doc. CRC/C/29, 1994), para. 172; *the United Kingdom of Great-Britain and Northern Ireland* (UN Doc. CRC/C/38, 1995), para. 234; *Nicaragua* (UN Doc. CRC/C/43, 1995), para. 57; *Canada* (UN Doc. CRC/C/43, 1995), para. 87; *Belgium* (UN Doc. CRC/C/43, 1995), para. 113; and *Germany* (UN Doc. CRC/C/46, 1995), para. 105.

[145] *E.g.* CRC Committee, *Concluding Observations: the United Kingdom of Great-Britain and Northern Ireland* (UN Doc. CRC/C/38, 1995), para. 234; and *Belgium* (UN Doc. CRC/C/43, 1995), para. 112.

[146] *E.g.* CRC Committee, *Concluding Observations: the Holy See* (UN Doc. CRC/C/46, 1995), para. 183.

[147] CESCR Committee, *General Comment No. 13 on the Right to Education* (UN Doc. E/C.12/1999/10, 1999), para. 6.

[148] See P. Meyer-Bisch, *The right to education in the context of cultural rights* (UN Doc. E/C.12/1998/17, 1998), para. 12.

[149] CESCR Committee, *General Comment No. 13 on the Right to Education* (UN Doc. E/C.12/1999/10, 1999), para. 9; Article 5 of the World Declaration on Education for All, adopted in 1990 in Jomtien (Thailand), *o.c.* (note 42).

basic learning content (such as knowledge, skills, values and attitudes) required by human beings to be able to survive, to develop their full capacities, to live and work in dignity, to participate fully in development, to improve the quality of their lives, to make informed decisions, and to continue learning.[150]

At secondary level, the basic learning skills should be completed and the foundations for life-long learning and human development should be consolidated.[151] At this level, students should be prepared for vocational and higher educational opportunities.[152]

At the level of higher education, the academic freedom of the staff and students has been emphasized. Academic freedom includes among others the freedom to transmit knowledge and ideas through teaching. This freedom applies to all levels of education but is especially important at the higher level as it is especially at this level that this freedom is undermined by political and other pressures.[153] The enjoyment of academic freedom carries with it the obligation for the State to ensure that the substance of education complies with this freedom.

1.1.6 *Forms of Education*

21. At the level of secondary and higher education, Article 28(1) requires that 'different forms of education' should be made available and accessible.

Article 28(1)(b) obliges the States to encourage the development of 'different forms of secondary education, including general and vocational education'. According to the CESCR Committee, this implies that the States should foresee flexible curricula and varied delivery systems to respond to the needs of students in different social and cultural settings.[154] General instruction and vocational education are expressly mentioned as forms of education to be made available. General instruction presumably refers to

---

[150] Article 1 of the World Declaration on Education for All, adopted in 1990 in Jomtien (Thailand), *o.c.* (note 42).

[151] The notions 'primary education' and 'basic education' are thus not synonymous. Although primary education is the core of basic education, basic education goes beyond the level of primary education; it is continued at the level of secondary education and also encompasses 'second chance' primary education of adults as well as pre-primary education. (K. Tomaševski, *Preliminary report of the Special Rapporteur on the right to education*, (UN Doc. E/CN.4/1999/49, 1998), para. 15 and UNICEF, *UNICEF strategies in basic education*, (UN Doc. E/ICEF/1995/16), para. 6).

[152] CESCR Committee, *General Comment No. 13 on the Right to Education* (UN Doc. E/C.12/1999/10, 1999), para. 12.

[153] *Ibid.*, paras. 38–39.

[154] *Ibid.*, para. 12.

the more traditional courses, such as mathematics, languages, history, geography etc. Vocational education is defined by UNESCO as 'those aspects of the educational process involving, in addition to general education, the study of technologies and related sciences and the acquisition of practical skills, know-how, attitudes and understanding relating to occupations in the various sectors of economic and social life'.[155] The explicit reference to vocational education is based on the belief that an introduction to the labour market forms an essential component of education. Therefore, vocational education should not merely be confined to specific programmes (as under Article 28(1)(d)) but should be understood as a component of the general education system.[156] Specific indications as to the contents of vocational education can be found in General Comment No. 13 on the Right to Education of the CESCR Committee,[157] Article 3 of the UNESCO Convention on Technical and Vocational Education[158] and in the Revised UNESCO Recommendation concerning technical and vocational education.[159]

The word 'including' in Article 28(1)(b) suggests a non-exhaustive enumeration.[160] Next to general and vocational education, other forms should exist. In its concluding observations, the CRC Committee often encourages the states to develop alternative educational programmes,[161] responding to the needs of the child within his or her social setting. Herewith the Committee refers *inter alia* to the special measures the government has to take in order to ensure the right to education of vulnerable groups (*cf. infra* No. 26 and 34). Although Article 28(1)(b) requires quite a large supply of forms at the level of secondary education, the CRC still offers a weaker protection in this regard than Article 13(2)(b) of the CESCR.[162] The obligation assumed under

---

[155] Article 1 of the UNESCO Convention on Technical and Vocational Education, adopted on 10 November 1989.

[156] CESCR Committee, *General Comment No. 13 on the Right to Education* (UN Doc. E/C.12/1999/10, 1999), para. 16. See also Article 2 and Articles 19–24 of the UNESCO Recommendation concerning technical and vocational education (1974), revised on 2 November 2001.

[157] CESCR Committee, *General Comment No. 13 on the Right to Education* (UN Doc. E/C.12/1999/10, 1999), para. 16.

[158] UNESCO Convention on Technical and Vocational Education, adopted on 10 November 1989.

[159] UNESCO Recommendation concerning technical and vocational education (1974), revised on 2 November 2001.

[160] The *Travaux Préparatoires* show that the former term 'both' was replaced by 'including' in order to avoid the exclusion of other forms of education: *Travaux Préparatoires* (UN Doc. E/CN.4/1989/WG.1/CRP.1, 1989), p. 33.

[161] *E.g.* CRC Committee, *Concluding Observations: Bulgaria* (UN Doc. CRC/C/62, 1997), para. 41; and *Slovenia* (UN Doc. CRC/C/50, 1996), para. 208; see also CESCR Committee, *General Comment No. 13 on the Right to Education* (UN Doc. E/C.12/1999/10, 1999), para. 12.

[162] D. Hodgson, *l.c.* (note 18), pp. 244–245; see also S. Detrick, *A Commentary on the United Nations Convention on the Rights of the Child*, *o.c.* (note 101), p. 481.

the latter provision to make secondary education in its different forms, including technical and vocational secondary education, generally accessible to all by every appropriate means logically encompasses the obligation to 'develop' different forms of secondary education. This wording implies an obligation, stronger than the one to merely 'encourage the development of' different forms of secondary education, as assumed under Article 28(1)(b) of the CRC.

As far as higher education is concerned, the CESCR Committee points out that, although the text of the provision regarding higher education does not include a reference to 'different forms' of education—as is the case in the paragraph regarding secondary education—also higher education has to be available in different forms. The same counts for 'vocational education', which forms an integral component of all levels of education, including higher education.[163] These interpretations may be read into the text of Article 28(1)(c) of the CRC, being largely drawn up along the lines of the equivalent CESCR-provision.

1.1.7 *Educational and Vocational Information and Guidance*

22. Article 28(1)(d) obliges the States to 'make educational and vocational information and guidance available and accessible to all children'. This provision is unique in international human rights law. The European Social Charter is the only other human rights instrument, enshrining a similar right to vocational assistance (Articles 9 and 10). The Charter goes a step further than the CRC by guaranteeing a right to assistance free of charge. Other instruments – generally considered not to be part of the human rights code – have normalized the issue of vocational guidance and training since decades. In this sense the ILO Convention No. 142 concerning Vocational Guidance and Vocational Training in the Development of Human resources (1975)[164] and the Revised UNESCO Recommendation concerning technical and vocational education[165] are noteworthy.

[163] CESCR Committee, *General Comment No. 13 on the Right to Education* (UN Doc. E/C.12/1999/10, 1999), paras. 18 and 16. Given the fact that Article 26(1) of the UDHR states that 'technical and professional educational shall be made generally available', without specifying the level of education, one can assume that vocational education forms an integral element of all forms of education.

[164] ILO Convention No. 142 concerning Vocational Guidance and Vocational Training in the Development of Human Resources, adopted on 3 June 1975, entered into force 19 July 1977.

[165] UNESCO Recommendation concerning technical and vocational education (1974), revised on 2 November 2001.

23. Under Article 28(1)(d), States Parties should firstly make the information and guidance 'available' and secondly make it 'accessible', which requires an active policy from the States. As stated above under No. 21, the States Parties already have an obligation to make vocational education available and accessible at the secondary and higher level of education. The 'Educational and vocational information and guidance' under subparagraph (d) therefore presumably refers to activities outside the school setting. One could raise the question whether this subparagraph is not abundant, considering the fact that pupils will automatically be guided and informed at school about the range of vocational opportunities available to them. According to Hodgkin and Newell the inclusion of an extra obligation on the States to also provide this guidance and information outside the school system was necessary as schools may have narrow expectations about what children will do in their future lives or be poorly informed about changing opportunities and requirements in terms of vocation.[166]

States Parties should make the educational and vocational information and guidance accessible to all. The obligation under subparagraph (d) indeed falls under the general obligation regarding equal opportunities in Article 28(1) (*cf. infra* No. 28 et seq.). Educational and vocational training and guidance should therefore also reach groups that are often excluded, such as women and disabled people.[167] The CRC Committee hence stresses that vocational education should also be promoted for disabled children[168] and juvenile offenders.[169] Also for young people and children who have missed out in educational opportunities, the importance of vocational training is emphasized.[170]

24. The content of the terms 'educational' and 'vocational' is not defined in Article 28(1)(d). The notion 'educational' presumably refers to information and guidance regarding the variety of opportunities as to disciplines and

[166] R. Hodgkin and P. Newell, *o.c.* (note 79), p. 420.

[167] This is in line with Article 9 of the Revised European Social Charter (1996), Article 2 of the UNESCO Convention on Technical and Vocational Education, adopted on 10 November 1989 and Article 3 of the ILO Convention No. 142 concerning Vocational Guidance and Vocational Training in the Development of Human resources, adopted on 3 June 1975, entered into force 19 July 1977.

[168] *E.g.* CRC Committee, *Concluding Observations: Cameroon* (UN Doc. CRC/C/111, 2001), para. 380; *Eritrea* (UN Doc. CRC/C/132, 2003), para. 72; and *India* (UN Doc. CRC/C/15/Add.228, 2004), para. 57. See also Articles 9, 10 and 15 of the Revised European Social Charter (1996).

[169] *E.g.* CRC Committee, *Concluding Observations: El Salvador* (UN Doc. CRC/C/15/Add.232, 2004), para. 58.

[170] *E.g.* CRC Committee, *Concluding Observations: Liberia* (UN Doc. CRC/C/15/Add.236, 2004), para. 57.

courses. The term 'vocational', on the other hand refers rather to information on career choices and opportunities. As stated above under No. 21, UNESCO and the CESCR Committee gave some indications as to what can be understood under 'vocational education'. ILO Convention 142 adds in Article 3 that 'such information and guidance shall cover the choice of an occupation, vocational training and related educational opportunities, the employment situation and employment prospects, promotion prospects, conditions of work, safety and hygiene at work, and other aspects of working life in the various sectors of economic, social and cultural activity and at all levels of responsibility'.[171]

The notion 'guidance' is defined by UNESCO as follows: 'Guidance (. . .) should be directed towards aiding all to make conscious and positive educational and occupational choices. It should ensure that individuals are provided with the prerequisites: (a) to become aware of their interests, abilities and special talents, and to help them frame a plan for life; (b) to pursue courses of education and training designed to realize their potential and fulfil their life plans; (c) to acquire flexibility in decision-making concerning their occupations, in the initial and later stages, for developing a satisfying career; (d) to facilitate transitions back and forth as needed, between education, training and the world of work'.[172] The 'information' that should accompany the guidance should give individuals 'a realistic view of the opportunities available, including trends in the labour market and employment structures, the environmental impact of various occupations, and what may be expected in terms of remuneration, career advancement and occupational mobility'.[173]

1.1.8 *School Attendance and Drop-out Rates*

25. A major global concern is that even in the year 2004 the global number of children not attending school remains at 121 million.[174] Article 28(1)(e) of the CRC provides the international legal basis to move a step closer to resolving this problem. It imposes an obligation to 'take measures to encourage

[171] Article 2 of ILO Convention No. 142 concerning Vocational Guidance and Vocational Training in the Development of Human Resources, adopted on 3 June 1975, entered into force 19 July 1977.

[172] Article 54 of the UNESCO Recommendation concerning technical and vocational education (1974), revised on 2 November 2001.

[173] Article 56 of the UNESCO Recommendation concerning technical and vocational education (1974), revised on 2 November 2001.

[174] C. Bellamy, *The State of the World's Children 2004, Girls, Education and Development* (New York/Geneva, UNICEF, 2004), p. 31.

regular attendance at schools and the reduction of drop-out rates'. This duty is innovative since it is omitted in the main international and regional human rights instruments. It specifies that it is not enough to have children merely registered at school, States Parties should also make sure that children *de facto* receive education by getting them and keeping them into school. Children with the highest rates of school drop-out tend to come from the groups generally discriminated against in education, such as girls, children from rural areas, children from minority groups or from the indigenous populations etc. (*cf. infra* No. 34).

26. The 'measures' the States Parties should take in order to encourage regular attendance at schools and the reduction of drop-out rates, should be of a positive nature. The drafters of the CRC stated that they did not want to approach the problem of irregular school attendance in a repressive way.[175]

As regards the kind of measures the States should take, the CRC Committee makes various recommendations according to the underlying cause of irregular school attendance and early school drop-out. When poverty is the underlying cause, the Committee encourages the States *inter alia* to take measures such as to initiate an analysis of child poverty as well as to provide for meals and health care at schools.[176] Girls drop out easier than boys for various reasons, including early marriage, teenage pregnancy, tradition, and violence and sexual harassment in the school setting.[177] In order to prevent girls dropping out of school because of pregnancy, the Committee recommends to include sex education into the school curriculum,[178] to ensure that pregnant teenagers are given the opportunity to complete their education by not excluding them,[179] and to develop special educational pro-

---

[175] *Travaux Préparatoires* (UN Doc. E/CN.4/1989/48, 1989), para. 467; reproduced in S. Detrick (ed.), *The United Nations Convention on the Rights of the Child: A Guide to the "Travaux Préparatoires"*, *o.c.* (note 88), p. 393.

[176] *E.g.* CRC Committee, *Concluding Observations: Grenada* (UN Doc. CRC/C/94, 2000), para. 408.

[177] In 2004, still millions more girls than boys are dropping out of primary school each year. 70 countries have girls' attendance and enrolment rates of less than 85 percent: See C. Bellamy, *The State of the World's Children 2004, Girls, Education and Development*, *o.c.* (note 174), pp. 33–34.

[178] *E.g.* CRC Committee, *Concluding Observations: Uruguay* (UN Doc. CRC/C/50, 1996), paras. 109 and 119. This recommendation is in line with the findings of the Special Rapporteur on the right to education: see K. Tomaševski, *The Right to education, Annual Report of the Special Rapporteur on the right to education 2003* (UN Doc. E/CN.4/2004/45, 2004), paras. 35–42.

[179] CRC Committee, *General Comment No. 4: Adolescent health and development in the context of the Convention on the Rights of the Child* (UN Doc. CRC/GC/2003/4, 2003), para. 31. See also *E.g.* CRC Committee, *Concluding Observations: Mozambique* (UN Doc. CRC/C/114, 2002), para. 306;

grammes for them.[180] Where violence or sexual abuse contribute to absenteeism and poor classroom performance of especially girls, the CRC Committee repeatedly emphasised that schools have to be safe and secure.[181] A high rate of school drop-out of children belonging to a minority can be dealt with by among others organising multilingual education (*cf. infra* No. 34 and 37),[182] and adapted programmes, such as mobile schools for children of nomads.[183] The problem of early school drop-out can also be caused by an irrelevant or unadjusted[184] school curriculum, incapability of the teachers or a repressive disciplinary system. In order to resolve this problem, the CRC Committee encourages active participation of pupils[185] as well as of the parents and collectivities (more specifically ethnic minorities)[186] in educational settings. Another effective method to increase the relevance of the curriculum and hence to combat school drop-out is the provision of better vocational education.[187]

Guyana (UN Doc. CRC/C/15/Add.224, 2004), para. 48; *Chile* (UN Doc. CRC/C/114, 2002), para. 370, and *New Zealand* (UN Doc. CRC/C/133, 2004), para. 156. This viewpoint is in line with Article 11(6) of the African Charter on the Rights and Welfare of the Child (1990), and with the recommendations of the Special Rapporteur on the Right to Education: K. Tomaševski, *Progress Report of the Special Rapporteur on the Right to Education 1999/25* (UN Doc. E/CN.4/2000/6, 2000), paras. 56–60.

[180] *E.g.* CRC Committee, *Concluding Observations: the United Kingdom of Great Britain and Northern Ireland* (UN Doc. CRC/C/121, 2002), para. 140.

[181] CRC Committee, *General Comment No. 3: HIV/AIDS and the rights of the child* (UN Doc. CRC/GC/2003/3, 2003), para. 19; CRC Committee, *General Comment No. 4: Adolescent health and development in the context of the Convention on the Rights of the Child* (UN Doc. CRC/GC/2003/4, 2003), para. 17. See also *E.g.* CRC Committee, *Concluding Observations: Democratic Republic of the Congo* (UN Doc. CRC/C/15/Add.153, 2001), paras. 60–61; and *United Republic of Tanzania* (UN Doc. CRC/C/15/Add.156, 2001), para. 57.

[182] *E.g.* CRC Committee, *Concluding Observations: Guatemala* (UN Doc. CRC/C/108, 2001), para. 274; *the Central African Republic* (UN Doc. CRC/C/100, 2000), paras. 467–468; *Slovakia* (UN Doc. CRC/C/100, 2000), paras. 590–591; *Georgia* (UN Doc. CRC/C/97, 2000), paras. 128–129; *Suriname* (UN Doc. CRC/C/97, 2000), paras. 499–500; and *the former Yugoslav Republic of Macedonia* (UN Doc. CRC/C/94, 2000), paras. 282–283.

[183] *E.g.* CRC Committee, Summary Records of the dialogue with *Mongolia* (UN Doc. CRC/C/265, 1996), para. 41.

[184] *E.g.* CRC Committee, *Concluding Observations: Costa Rica* (UN Doc. CRC/C/94, 2000), para. 233.

[185] *E.g.* CRC Committee, *Concluding Observations: Cameroon* (UN Doc. CRC/C/111, 2001), para. 380; *Turkey* (UN Doc. CRC/C/108, 2001), para. 136; *Saudi-Arabia* (UN Doc. CRC/C/103, 2001), para. 414; and *the Netherlands Antilles* (UN Doc. CRC/C/118, 2002), para. 576.

[186] *E.g.* CRC Committee, *Concluding Observations: Uzbekistan* (UN Doc. CRC/C/111, 2001), para. 581; and *Jordan* (UN Doc. CRC/C/97, 2000), para. 200.

[187] R. Hodgkin and P. Newell, *o.c.* (note 79), p. 422. *E.g.* CRC Committee, *Concluding Observations: Burundi* (UN Doc. CRC/C/15/Add.133, 2000), para. 65; and *Liberia* (UN Doc. CRC/C/15/Add.236, 2004), para. 57.

27. The level of education at which the States should promote school attendance is not specified in the CRC. The *Travaux Préparatoires* only expose a point of discussion between the United States, being of the opinion that such measures should be limited to primary and secondary education, and France, wanting to protect students in higher education against a lack of self-discipline.[188] This argument, however, did not result into specific indications regarding the levels of education in the text of Article 28(1)(e). From the holdings of the CRC Committee, it can be derived that States should take such measures at both primary and secondary level.[189]

1.2 *The Right to Equal Access to and Equal Opportunities in Education*

28. Throughout history governments tended and still do use the system of education to systematically discriminate against certain vulnerable groups, such as women, black people and ethnic, religious and linguistic minorities. Education indeed proved to be an effective means to retain inequality. It could, however, also be a means to eliminate inequality. Because education can serve these two mutually contradictory purposes, the drafters of the CRC decided to put a strong emphasis on equality in education by reconfirming the general non-discrimination principle of Article 2(1) of the CRC in the *chapeau* of Article 28(1) of the CRC and hence making all other aspects of the right to education dependent upon it. States Parties to the CRC should thus make education available and accessible 'on the basis of equal opportunities'. It concerns an accessory obligation, putting an extra protection layer around the subjective rights in Article 28(1).[190] The reference to 'equal opportunities' is a stronger formulation than the one in Article 2(1) of the CRC as it more explicitly obliges the States not only to ensure formal equality but also substantive equality, which often requires affirmative action policies.

---

[188] *Travaux Préparatoires* (UN Doc. E/CN.4/1989/48, 1989), para. 468; reproduced in S. Detrick (ed.), *The United Nations Convention on the Rights of the Child: A Guide to the "Travaux Préparatoires"*, *o.c.* (note 88), pp. 393–394.

[189] *E.g.* CRC Committee, *Concluding Observations: Oman* (UN Doc. CRC/C/111, 2001), paras. 191–192; *Ecuador* (UN Doc. CRC/C/80, 1998), para. 49; *Kyrgyztan* (UN Doc. CRC/C/97, 2000), paras. 318–319; *Portugal* (UN Doc. CRC/C/111, 2001), paras. 246–247; and *Jordan* (UN Doc. CRC/C/97, 2000), para. 200.

[190] See Nowak's statements regarding the equivalent provisions in the CCPR (Article 2(1)): M. Nowak, *U.N. Covenant on Civil and Political Rights—CCPR Commentary*, *o.c.* (note 13), p. 43, para. 31.

29. The *prohibited grounds* for distinctions in education can in the first place be found in Article 2(1) of the CRC: a difference in treatment on the basis of the child's or his or her parent's or legal guardian's race, colour, sex, language, religion, political or other opinion, national, ethnic or social origin, property, disability, birth or other status does not comply with the Convention. These grounds are similar to those stated in Article 2(1) of the CESCR and Article 2(1) of the CCPR, with the addition of ethnic origin and disability.[191] The notion 'other status' is presumably not a wide-open concept but rather restricted to embrace only those categories that are similar to the listed ones. This follows from the fact that the Human Rights Committee as well as the CESCR Committee interpret the equivalent articles[192] in the respective Conventions in this sense.[193] In its concluding observations to the States Parties reports, the CRC Committee has identified several grounds which could fall under the notion 'other status': sexual orientation, place of residence (distinctions between different provinces/regions,[194] homeless, rural, abandoned, displaced etc.), children involved in the juvenile justice system, in armed conflict, etc.[195]

30. The prohibition of discrimination in '*education*' refers, according to Article 1(2) of the UNESCO Convention against Discrimination in Education[196]—being the most specific convention on discrimination in education—, to all educational levels and regards the access to education, the standard and quality of the education and the conditions under which it is given.

---

[191] Similar discrimination grounds can be found in Article 1(1) of the UNESCO Convention against Discrimination in Education (1960). Gender discrimination in education is equally prohibited by Article 10 of the CEDAW (1979). Racial discrimination in education is equally prohibited by Article 5(e)(v) of the CERD (1965). Equal opportunities for indigenous and tribal people in education are guaranteed in part VI of the ILO Convention No. 169 concerning Indigenous and Tribal Peoples in Independent Countries (1989).

[192] Article 2(1) of the CESCR and Article 2(1) of the CCPR.

[193] B. Abramson, *l.c.* (note 12), p. 64.

[194] In a federal State, the education system sometimes belongs to the competence of the regions and could therefore differ according to the region. The CRC Committee stressed that it is up to the federal Government to ensure that equal protection is given to children in all different regions of that State. *E.g.* CRC Committee, *Concluding Observations: Belgium* (UN Doc. CRC/C/15/Add.178, 2002), para. 10. See also CESCR Committee, *General Comment No. 13 on the Right to Education* (UN Doc. E/C.12/1999/10, 1999), para. 35.

[195] For a complete list of the grounds for discrimination, identified by the CRC Committee, see R. Hodgkin and P. Newell, *o.c.* (note 79), p. 28.

[196] UNESCO Convention against Discrimination in Education, adopted on 14 December 1960, entered into force 22 May 1962 (hereinafter often referred to as 'the UNESCO Convention'). The Convention has, however, been ratified by 89 States only.

31. '*Discrimination*' in education is, according to Article 1(1) of the UNESCO Convention, any distinction, exclusion, limitation or preference on prohibited grounds that has the purpose of effect of nullifying or impairing equality of treatment in education. In particular, the Convention aims at eradicating practices of depriving any person or group access to education, of limiting any person or group to education of an inferior standard, of maintaining separate educational systems for any person or group and of imposing on any person or group conditions which are incompatible with human dignity.

32. Not every unequal treatment constitutes discrimination. Distinctions are prohibited as discriminatory only when they are not supported by reasonable and objective criteria.[197] The CESCR Committee recognises the legitimacy of affirmative actions[198] as well as of separate educational systems or institutions for certain groups in some circumstances.[199] This is in line with Article 2 of the UNESCO Convention, which permits the establishment or maintenance of separate education systems for pupils of the two sexes as well as for religious or linguistic reasons. The deduction of a prohibition of single-sex schools from Article 28(1) of the CRC is therefore not obvious. Firstly, the phrasing of the provision is not sufficiently clear and precise to deduct such a prohibition. Secondly, the UNESCO Convention and the holdings of the CESCR Committee point at the opposite. The CRC Committee, nevertheless, states in its General Comment No. 1 that 'While denying a child's access to educational opportunities is primarily a matter which relates to Article 28 of the Convention, there are many ways in which failure to comply with the principles contained in Article 29(1) can have a similar effect. To take an extreme example, gender discrimination can be reinforced by practices such as a curriculum which is inconsistent with the principles contained of gender equality, by arrangements which limit the benefits girls can obtain from the educational opportunities offered, and by unsafe or unfriendly environments which discourage girls' participation'.[200] If the phrase 'access to educational opportunities' means 'access to educational institutions', one could conclude that the CRC Committee proclaims a pro-

---

[197] See Nowak's statements regarding the equivalent provisions in the CCPR (Article 2(1)): M. Nowak, *U.N. Covenant on Civil and Political Rights—CCPR Commentary*, *o.c.* (note 13), p. 44, para. 32.

[198] CESCR Committee, *General Comment No. 13 on the Right to Education* (UN Doc. E/C.12/1999/10, 1999), para. 32.

[199] *Ibid.*, para. 33.

[200] CRC Committee, *General Comment No. 1 on the Aims of Education* (UN Doc. CRC/GC/2001/1, 2001), para. 10.

hibition of distinction in access to schools on the basis of gender. This interpretation would be in line with Article 10(c) of the CEDAW, which explicitly encourages coeducation. The current possibly opposite views of both UN Committees and the apparent contradictory international standards on the issue of coeducation, make it impossible to give a clear answer to the question whether Article 28(1) of the CRC proscribes single-sex schools.

33. In terms of *States obligations*, the non-discrimination principle of the CRC obliges the governments (1) to respect the equality principle in public schools in legislation, policy and practice as to the several aspects of education (*e.g.* accessibility, free primary education, content/quality etc.); (2) to take protective measures in order to prevent or combat discrimination in education by third parties; and (3) to undertake an active policy in order to guarantee substantive equality.[201] More specific measures that could be undertaken to eliminate *de jure* and *de facto* discrimination can be derived from the enumeration of measures in Article 3 of the UNESCO Convention,[202] the *Limburg Principles*,[203] and from the CRC Committee's recommendations to fight discrimination of particularly vulnerable groups, which will be elaborated upon in the next paragraphs.

34. In general, the non-discrimination principle in Article 2, reconfirmed in Article 28(1), applies to *each child* within the jurisdiction of a State. It therefore extends to non-nationals, irrespective of their legal status.

---

[201] See F. Coomans, 'In search of the core content of the right to education', *l.c.* (note 3), pp. 245–246.

[202] Article 3 of the UNESCO Convention against Discrimination in Education (1960) lists the following measures:

(a) To abrogate any statutory provisions and any administrative instructions and to discontinue any administrative practices which involve discrimination in education;

(b) To, ensure, by legislation where necessary, that there is no discrimination in the admission of pupils to educational institutions;

(c) Not to allow any differences of treatment by the public authorities between nationals, except on the basis of merit or need, in the matter of school fees and the grant of scholarships or other forms of assistance to pupils and necessary permits and facilities for the pursuit of studies in foreign countries;

(d) Not to allow, in any form of assistance granted by the public authorities to educational institutions, any restrictions or preference based solely on the ground that pupils belong to a particular group;

(e) To give foreign nationals resident within their territory the same access to education as that given to their own nationals.

[203] The Limburg principles on the Implementation of the International Covenant on Economic, Social and Cultural Rights of 6 June 1986 (UN Doc. E/CN.4/1987/17, 1987), paras. 35–41; reproduced in *Human Rights Quarterly* 9, 1987, pp. 122–135.

The principle of equality implies moreover that special attention should be given to *specific groups*, which are particularly vulnerable to discrimination in education and which consequently require special policies. The type of education offered to these children should be geared to their specific educational needs. In other words, education has to be 'adaptable' to these children.[204]

It is clear that *girls* are disadvantaged in education and therefore deserve special attention. For more than a decade, gender parity in education has been a focal point at several international summits and conferences,[205] is mentioned among the Millennium Developments Goals, to be met partly in 2005,[206] and has constituted one of the main concerns of the Special Rapporteur on the right to education.[207] Nevertheless, the majority of the currently 121 million children not attending school are still girls.[208] Therefore, the CRC Committee continues to focus on girls' education as it has already repeatedly done in its concluding observations[209] and during a day of gen-

---

204 *Cf. supra* note 63.

205 This was the case during *inter alia* the 1990 World Conference on Education for All (Jomtien) (Article 3(3) of the World Declaration on Education for All, *o.c.* (note 42)); the 1990 World Summit for Children (Plan of Action for Implementing the World Declaration on the Survival, Protection and Development of Children in the 1990, para. 10); the 1995 World Conference on Women (Platform for Action, Beijing (UN Doc. A/CONF.177/20/Rev.1, 1996), paras. 263 and 279); the special session of the General Assembly in 2000 to follow up the World Conference on Women (Further actions and initiatives to implement the Beijing Declaration and Platform for Action (UN Doc. A/RES/S-23/3, 2000), paras. 9 and 10); and the 2000 World Education Forum (Dakar) (Articles 7(ii) and (v) and 8(vi) of the Dakar Framework for Action, *o.c.* (note 42)). See also K. Annan, *We the Children, Meeting the promises of the World Summit for Children*, *o.c.* (note 52), pp. 57–59 and 71, *i.e.* a preparatory document for the 2002 Special Session of the General Assembly on Children.

206 The elimination of gender disparity in primary and secondary education is aimed for by 2005, and at all levels by 2015. (UN Millenium Development Goals, http://www.un.org/millenniumgoals)

207 K. Tomaševski, *Preliminary report of the Special Rapporteur on the right to education* (UN Doc. E/CN.4/1999/49, 1998), paras. 9, 41, 53–56, 60, 73–74; K. Tomaševski, *Progress Report of the Special Rapporteur on the Right to Education 1999/25* (UN Doc. E/CN.4/2000/6, 2000), paras. 56–60; K. Tomaševski, *Annual Report of the special Rapporteur on the Right to Education 2000/9* (UN Doc. E/CN.4/2001/52, 2001), paras. 7–8; K. Tomaševski, *Annual Report of the Special Rapporteur on the Right to Education 2001/29* (UN Doc. E/CN.4/2002/60, 2002), paras. 40–45; K. Tomaševski, *The Right to education, Annual Report of the Special Rapporteur on the right to education 2003* (UN Doc. E/CN.4/2004/45, 2004), paras. 31–34; and K. Tomaševski, *Education Denied*, *o.c.* (note 53), pp. 158–171.

208 C. Bellamy, *The State of the World's Children 2004, Girls, Education and Development*, *o.c.* (note 174), p. 31.

209 *E.g.* CRC Committee, *Concluding Observations: Egypt* (UN Doc. CRC/C/16, 1993), para. 104; *Pakistan* (UN Doc. CRC/C/29, 1994), para. 55; *Lebanon* (UN Doc. CRC/C/54, 1996), para. 50; *Saudi-Arabia* (UN Doc. CRC/C/103, 2001), paras. 413–414; *Mali* (UN Doc. CRC/C/90, 1999), para. 223; *Benin* (UN Doc. CRC/C/87, 1999), para. 159; *Irak* (UN Doc. CRC/C/80, 1998), para. 74; *Senegal* (UN Doc. CRC/C/46, 1995), paras. 126 and 139; *Pakistan* (UN Doc. CRC/C/29, 1994),

eral discussion on the girl child.[210] Among other things, the Committee emphasizes effective access to education for girls, addresses the importance of human rights education in the elimination of stereotypes,[211] and recommends measures increasing the awareness of the parents with regard to the gender gap.[212] As stated above, the CRC Committee also made several recommendations in order to prevent girls dropping out of school because of pregnancy and abuse at school (*cf. supra* No. 26). The recommendations of the CRC Committee regarding equal opportunities for girls in education are in line with Article 10 of the CEDAW. This Convention contains a number of specific positive obligations, including the elimination of any stereotyped concept of the roles of men and women, the encouragement of coeducation, the revision of text-books, the adaptation of teaching methods, the reduction of any gap in education existing between men and women and the reduction of female student drop-out rates.

Another special group having difficulties in exercising their education rights are *children living in rural areas*. This is due to a number of factors, including the administrative cost and difficulty of servicing remote areas, the small number of teachers prepared to live in the countryside, the dependence of farming families on child labour and the apparent irrelevance of the school curricula to rural lives.[213] The CRC Committee repetitively recommended the States Parties to give special attention to the education of these children.[214] In the case of Poland, for instance, the Committee recommended the government to ensure that rural areas are provided with additional funds to allow them to provide the same quality of education and level of extracurricular programmes as urban schools and to make sure that students from rural areas have access to scholarships that allow them to attend secondary education.[215]

---

paras. 41 and 55; *Djibouti* (UN Doc. CRC/C/97, 2000), para. 556; *Mozambique* (UN Doc. CRC/C/114, 2002), para. 306; and *Ethiopia* (UN Doc. CRC/C/103, 2001), para. 183.

[210] CRC Committee, *Day of General Discussion on the Girl Child* (UN Doc. CRC/C/38, 1995), paras. 289–290.

[211] *E.g.* CRC Committee, *Concluding Observations: El Salvador* (UN Doc. CRC/C/20, 1993), para. 93; *the Federal Republic of Yugoslavia (Serbia and Montenegro)* (UN Doc. CRC/C/50, 1996), para. 108; and *the Democratic People's Republic of Korea* (UN Doc. CRC/C/15/Add.239, 2004), para. 55.

[212] *E.g.* CRC Committee, *Concluding Observations: Egypt* (UN Doc. CRC/C/16, 1993), para. 104.

[213] R. Hodgkin and P. Newell, *o.c.* (note 79), p. 414.

[214] *E.g.* CRC Committee, *Concluding Observations: Jordan* (UN Doc. CRC/C/29, 1994), para. 131, *Colombia* (UN Doc. CRC/C/38, 1995), para. 96; *Yemen* (UN Doc. CRC/C/50, 1996), paras. 63 and 71; *Lesotho* (UN Doc. CRC/C/103, 2001), paras. 361–362; *Georgia* (UN Doc. CRC/C/97, 2000), para. 128; *Sierra Leone* (UN Doc. CRC/C/94, 2000), paras. 180–181; *Mexico* (UN Doc. CRC/C/90, 1999), para. 187; and *Poland* (UN Doc. CRC/C/121, 2002), para. 538.

[215] *E.g.* CRC Committee, *Concluding Observations: Poland* (UN Doc. CRC/C/121, 2002), para. 538.

Also discrimination against *children belonging to a minority*[216] or the *indigenous population*[217] was often a point of concern in the concluding observations of the CRC Committee as well as during its day of general discussion on the rights of indigenous children.[218] It is important for these children that education facilitates their integration in the wider society and at the same time positively reinforces their minority or indigenous identity.[219] The latter can be realised by among others the use of minority and indigenous languages in education. The Convention itself requires in its Article 30 that a child belonging to an ethnic, religious or linguistic minority or who is indigenous shall not be denied the right, in community with other members of his or her group, to enjoy his or her own culture, to profess and practice his or her own religion, or to use his or her own language.[220] Although this article does not explicitly provide the child with a right to education in his or her own language, the CRC Committee used it to stress the importance of multilingual education in the realisation of the right to education of children belonging to a minority or indigenous population.[221] This concern of the Committee is in line with Article 5 of the UNESCO Convention against Discrimination in Education, Article 4(3) of the Declaration on the

---

[216] *E.g.* CRC Committee, *Concluding Observations: China* (UN Doc. CRC/C/54, 1996), paras. 123 and 144; *Slovakia* (UN Doc. CRC/C/100, 2000), paras. 590–591; *the former Yugoslav Republic of Macedonia* (UN Doc. CRC/C/94, 2000), paras. 280–281; and *Spain* (UN Doc. CRC/C/118, 2002), paras. 509, 511 and 518.

[217] *E.g.* CRC Committee, *Concluding Observations: Canada* (UN Doc. CRC/C/43, 1995), paras. 85 and 94; and *Mexico* (UN Doc. CRC/C/90, 1999), para. 187.

[218] CRC Committee, *Day of General Discussion on the Rights of Indigenous Children* (UN Doc. CRC/C/133, 2003), paras. 608–624.

[219] See on this issue: H. Cullen, 'Education Rights or Minority Rights', *International Journal of Law and the Family* 7, 1993, pp. 143–177.

[220] This article is a copy of Article 27 of the CCPR, except that it extends the protection to indigenous children in addition to children of minorities.

[221] This follows from its reporting guidelines, which contain a reporting question as to the measures States have adopted to ensure that children may be taught in local, indigenous or minority languages: CRC Committee, *General Guidelines regarding the form and the contents of the periodic reports* (UN Doc. CRC/C/58, 1996), para. 106. States who fail in this regard are recommended by the CRC Committee to organise multilingual education: *E.g.* CRC Committee, *Concluding Observations: Guatemala* (UN Doc. CRC/C/54, 1996), para. 227; *Myanmar* (UN Doc. CRC/C/62, 1997), paras. 153 and 173; *the Central African Republic* (UN Doc. CRC/C/100, 2000), paras. 467–468; *Slovakia* (UN Doc. CRC/C/100, 2000), paras. 590–591; *Georgia* (UN Doc. CRC/C/97, 2000), paras. 128–129; *Suriname* (UN Doc. CRC/C/97, 2000), paras. 499–500; *the former Yugoslav Republic of Macedonia* (UN Doc. CRC/C/94, 2000), paras. 282–283; *Estonia* (UN Doc. CRC/C/124, 2003), para. 65; *the Federal Republic of Yugoslavia (Serbia and Montenegro)* (UN Doc. CRC/C/50, 1996), paras. 86, 97 and 108; *Colombia* (UN Doc. CRC/C/100, 2000), para. 375; *Guatemala* (UN Doc. CRC/C/108, 2001), para. 274; and *Belarus* (UN Doc. CRC/C/118, 2002), para. 250). See also CRC Committee, *Day of General Discussion on the Rights of Indigenous Children* (UN Doc. CRC/C/133, 2003), paras. 608–624.

Rights of Persons Belonging to National or Ethnic, Religious and Linguistic Minorities,[222] Article 28 of the ILO Convention No. 169 concerning Indigenous and Tribal Peoples in Independent Countries (1989), Article 8 of the European Charter for Regional or Minority Languages,[223] and Article 14 of the Framework Convention for the Protection of National Minorities.[224] The issue of education in minority languages has been elaborated upon below under No. 37.

The Committee also repeatedly expressed its concern about the discrimination in education of *internally displaced children, refugee children*[225] and *children of immigrants*.[226] It welcomed the establishment of a special programme for teachers at all levels on education for immigrants,[227] and recommended the governments to adopt comprehensive legislation to ensure adequate protection of refugee and asylum-seeking children, including in the field of education.[228] The latter recommendation is in line with Article 22 of the Convention relating to the Status of Refugees (1951).[229]

Children affected by armed conflicts are another group that is often denied rights to education. The CRC Committee urged States to make sure that also in times of war education is provided to children in both rural and urban areas.[230] States are encouraged to take effective measures to ensure that these children can be reintegrated in the education system, including through

---

[222] Declaration on the Rights of Persons Belonging to National or Ethnic, Religious and Linguistic Minorities, adopted on 18 December 1992 (UN Doc. A/RES/47/135).

[223] European Charter for Regional or Minority Languages, adopted by the Council of Europe on 5 November 1992, entered into force 1 March 1998.

[224] Framework Convention for the Protection of National Minorities, adopted by the Council of Europe on 1 February 1995, entered into force 1 February 1998.

[225] *E.g.* CRC Committee, *Concluding Observations: Norway* (UN Doc. CRC/C/29, 1994), para. 177; *Denmark* (UN Doc. CRC/C/38, 1995), para. 199; *Belgium* (UN Doc. CRC/C/43, 1995), para. 104; *Sri Lanka* (UN Doc. CRC/C/43, 1995), paras. 154 and 172; *Djibouti* (UN Doc. CRC/C/97, 2000), para. 556; *Burundi* (UN Doc. CRC/C/100, 2000), paras. 152–153; *Finland* (UN Doc. CRC/C/100, 2000), para. 76; and *Spain* (UN Doc. CRC/C/118, 2002), paras. 512–513.

[226] *E.g.* CRC Committee, *Concluding Observations: Iceland* (UN Doc. CRC/C/132, 2003), paras. 512–513.

[227] *E.g.* CRC Committee, *Concluding Observations: Iceland* (UN Doc. CRC/C/50, 1996), para. 132.

[228] *E.g.* CRC Committee, *Concluding Observations: India* (UN Doc. CRC/C/15/Add.228, 2004), paras. 70–71; *South Africa* (UN Doc. CRC/C/15/Add.122, 2000), para. 35; and *Norway* (UN Doc. CRC/C/15/Add.126, 2000), paras. 48 and 50.

[229] This article provides that the governments 'shall accord to refugees the same treatment as is accorded to nationals with respect to elementary education', and in respect for all other types and levels of education 'treatment as favourable as possible, and, in any event, not less favourable than that accorded to aliens generally in the same circumstances'.

[230] *E.g.* CRC Committee, *Concluding Observations: Mozambique* (UN Doc. CRC/C/114, 2002), para. 312. See also CRC Committee, *Day of General Discussion on children in armed conflict* (UN Doc. CRC/C/10, 1992), para. 73.

the provision of non-formal education programmes and by prioritising a rehabilitation of school buildings and facilities in these regions.[231] As far as child soldiers are concerned, the Committee advises the States to set up programmes of rehabilitation and reintegration.[232]

Further, also *children with disabilities* are entitled to education that maximizes their potential, but are in reality often discriminated against. Article 23(3) of the CRC therefore explicitly imposes obligations on the States to take measures that ensure that disabled children have effective access to and receive education.[233] The CRC Committee recommended to establish special education programmes for children with disabilities[234] and, where feasible, to integrate them into mainstream schools.[235] According to Hodgkin and Newell, the phrase 'in a manner conducive to the child's achieving the fullest possible social integration' in Article 23(3) of the CRC reveals a preference for the latter option, *i.e.* inclusive education.[236] This preference is in line with a general trend. Courts in a variety of countries proclaim inclusiveness, *i.e.* the integration of learners with disabilities in general schools.[237] Inclusive education, however, requires that teachers and schools have to

---

[231] *E.g.* CRC Committee, *Concluding Observations: Sri Lanka* (UN Doc. CRC/C/132, 2003), para. 272; *Indonesia* (UN Doc. CRC/C/15/Add.223, 2004), para. 72; and *Myanmar* (UN Doc. CRC/C/15/Add.237, 2004), para. 67.

[232] *E.g.* CRC Committee, *Concluding Observations: Colombia* (UN Doc. CRC/C/100, 2000), para. 379.

[233] See also Article 15(1) of the European Social Charter; Principle 6 of the Declaration on the Rights of Disabled Persons, adopted on 9 December 1975; and Rule 6 of the Standard Rules on the Equalization of Opportunities for Persons with Disabilities, adopted on 20 December 1993 (UN Doc. A/RES/48/96).

[234] However, laws which compulsory segregate disabled children in separate institutions for education should be amended: CRC Committee, *Day of General Discussion on Children with Disabilities* (UN Doc. CRC/C/66, 1997), Annex V, para. 338 (d).

[235] *E.g.* CRC Committee, *Concluding Observations: Azerbaijan* (UN Doc. CRC/C/66, 1997), para. 296; *the United Kingdom of Great Britain and Northern Ireland—Isle of Man* (UN Doc. CRC/C/100, 2000), para. 195; *Niger* (UN Doc. CRC/C/118, 2002), paras. 179–180; *Switzerland* (UN Doc. CRC/C/118, 2002), para. 347; *Dominica* (UN Doc. CRC/C/15/Add.238, 2004, para. 37; *Yemen* (UN Doc. CRC/C/50, 1996), paras. 63 and 71; *Korea* (UN Doc. CRC/C/50, 1996), para. 171; *Burundi* (UN Doc. CRC/C/100, 2000), paras. 138 and 150; *Colombia* (UN Doc. CRC/C/100, 2000), para. 373; *Tunisia* (UN Doc. CRC/C/118, 2002), paras. 291–292; and *New Zealand* (UN Doc. CRC/C/133, 2004), para. 152. With regard to adolescents, see CRC Committee, *General Comment No. 4: Adolescent health and development in the context of the Convention on the Rights of the Child* (UN Doc. CRC/GC/2003/4, 2003), para. 19.

[236] R. Hodgkin and P. Newell, *o.c.* (note 79), p. 415.

[237] K. Tomaševski, *Right to Education Primer 3: Human rights obligations: making education available, accessible, acceptable and adaptable*, *o.c.* (note 3), p. 32. See also Rule 6 of the Standard Rules on the Equalization of Opportunities for Persons with Disabilities, adopted on 20 December 1993 (UN Doc. A/RES/48/96).

adapt to learners with divergent abilities and needs.[238] The CRC Committee takes these financial and practical consequences into account and therefore specifies that this should be done where feasible only.

Juvenile offenders are another category, which is often denied appropriate education. Therefore Article 40(4) of the CRC explicitly guarantees that educational programmes must be made available for juvenile delinquents. The CRC Committee urges the States to take all the necessary measures to ensure that children deprived of their liberty have a statutory right to education and *de facto* continue to have education.[239]

Street children habitually have problems exercising their right to education. The CRC Committee encourages the States to ensure that these children continue to have access to education and encourages that States to adapt the school curricula to these children.[240]

Regarding *working children*, the CRC Committee stresses—in accordance with Article 32 of the CRC—that child labour may not interfere with the child's education. To this end, States are recommended to prevent and eliminate child labour[241] and to ensure that the minimum age of employment corresponds to the end of compulsory education.[242] The link between the

---

[238] CESCR Committee, *General Comment No. 5: Persons with disabilities (1994)* (UN Doc. HRI/GEN/1/Rev.7, 2004), p. 32, para. 35.

[239] *E.g.* CRC Committee, *Concluding Observations: the Seychelles* (UN Doc. CRC/C/121, 2002), para. 215; *Luxembourg* (UN Doc. CRC/C/79, 1998), para. 280; *Paraguay* (UN Doc. CRC/C/111, 2001), para. 521; *the United Kingdom of Great Britain and Northern Ireland* (UN Doc. CRC/C/121, 2002), para. 154, *Ukraine* (UN Doc. CRC/C/121, 2002), para. 364; *El Salvador* (UN Doc. CRC/C/15/Add.232, 2004), para. 58.

[240] *E.g.* CRC Committee, *Concluding Observations: Burundi* (UN Doc. CRC/C/100, 2000), para. 155; *Gabon* (UN Doc. CRC/C/114, 2002), para. 239; *Mozambique* (UN Doc. CRC/C/114, 2002), para. 318; *Zambia* (UN Doc. CRC/C/132, 2003), para. 220; *Haiti* (UN Doc. CRC/C/124, 2003), para. 445; *Sudan* (UN Doc. CRC/C/121, 2002), para. 287; *India* (CRC/C/15/Add.228, para. 77), *Pakistan* (UN Doc. CRC/C/133, 2004), para. 245; and *Madagascar* (UN Doc. CRC/C/133, 2004), para. 315.

[241] *E.g.* CRC Committee, *Concluding Observations: Mauritius* (UN Doc. CRC/C/50, 1996), para. 189; *France* (UN Doc. CRC/C/29, 1994), para. 105; and *Bangladesh* (UN Doc. CRC/C/66, 1997), para. 167.

[242] *E.g.* CRC Committee, *Concluding Observations: Tunisia* (UN Doc. CRC/C/43, 1995), para. 125; *Guatemala* (UN Doc. CRC/C/54, 1996), paras. 205 and 231; and *Dominica* (UN Doc. CRC/C/15/Add.238, 2004), para. 20. With regard to adolescents, see CRC Committee, *General Comment No. 4: Adolescent health and development in the context of the Convention on the Rights of the Child* (UN Doc. CRC/GC/2003/4, 2003), para. 18.

The minimum age for employment may also not be established long after the end of compulsory education as this may render children who finished compulsory education but did not yet attain the minimum age for employment vulnerable to the risk of economic exploitation: *E.g.* CRC Committee, *Concluding Observations: Nicaragua* (UN Doc. CRC/C/43, 1995), para. 41; and *Ukraine* (UN Doc. CRC/C/46, 1995), paras. 54 and 63. See also the findings of the

age for completion of compulsory education and the minimum age for employment has also been stressed in Article 2(3) of the ILO Convention No. 38 and in Article 7(3) of the European Social Charter (1961 (revised 1996)). Also the Special Rapporteur on the right to education has exerted a great deal of effort to further acceptance of this link.[243] The CRC Committee suggests that the States should at least provide in educational programmes that are adapted to working children;[244] a view which is shared by the Special Rapporteur on the right to education.[245]

In relation to the education of *children affected by HIV/AIDS*, the CRC Committee recommended States Parties to make adequate provision to ensure that infected children can stay in school and to ensure the qualified replacement of sick teachers so that the children's regular attendance at school is not affected.[246] Also the impact of the death of a relative in terms of the children's reduced access to education should be minimized.[247] The Committee further recommended to include HIV/AIDS issues, including teaching of life-skills, in school curricula.[248]

Further, the CRC Committee urged some States to further develop services for *children with learning difficulties*.[249]

Special Rapporteur on the right to education: K. Tomaševski, *Annual Report of the special Rapporteur on the Right to Education 2000/9* (UN Doc. E/CN.4/2001/52, 2001), para. 28; K. Tomaševski, *Annual Report of the special Rapporteur on the Right to Education 2002/23* (UN Doc. E/CN.4/2003/9, 2003), para. 12.

[243] K. Tomaševski, *Progress Report of the Special Rapporteur on the Right to Education 1999/25*, (UN Doc. E/CN.4/2000/6, 2000), paras. 61–62; K. Tomaševski, *Annual Report of the special Rapporteur on the Right to Education 2000/9* (UN Doc. E/CN.4/2001/52, 2001), para. 28; K. Tomaševski, *Annual Report of the special Rapporteur on the Right to Education 2002/23* (UN Doc. E/CN.4/2003/9, 2003), paras. 12–13.

[244] *E.g.* CRC Committee, *Concluding Observations: Venezuela* (UN Doc. CRC/C/90, 1999), para. 55; *Honduras* (UN Doc. CRC/C/34, 1994), para. 58; *Guinea-Bissau* (UN Doc. CRC/C/118, 2002), para. 81; and *Sudan* (UN Doc. CRC/C/121, 2002), para. 283.

[245] K. Tomaševski, *Progress Report of the Special Rapporteur on the Right to Education 1999/25* (UN Doc. E/CN.4/2000/6, 2000), paras. 64–65.

[246] CRC Committee, *General Comment No. 3: HIV/AIDS and the rights of the child* (UN Doc. CRC/GC/2003/3, 2003), para. 18.

[247] *E.g.* CRC Committee, *Concluding Observations: the Central African Republic* (UN Doc. CRC/C/100, 2000), para. 454; *Zambia* (UN Doc. CRC/C/132, 2003), para. 202; and *India* (UN Doc. CRC/C/15/Add.228, 2004), para. 55.

[248] CRC Committee, *General Comment No. 3: HIV/AIDS and the rights of the child* (UN Doc. CRC/GC/2003/3, 2003), paras. 17–18; and CRC Committee, *Day of General Discussion on Children living in a World with AIDS* (UN Doc. CRC/C/79, 1998), Annex VI, para. 243.

[249] *E.g.* CRC Committee, *Concluding Observations: Germany* (UN Doc. CRC/C/15/Add.226, 2004), para. 53.

1.3 *The Freedom to Choose Education*

35. Some traditional education rights, which should ensure that education is 'acceptable' to parents, are not included in Article 28. It concerns mainly the liberty of the parents to choose the kind of education for their child according to their religious and moral convictions,[250] and their freedom to choose another school for their children than a State-run school.[251]

36. As far as the right of the parents to have their religious and moral convictions respected in the education of their child is concerned, no explicit reference can be found in Article 28, nor in any other article of the CRC. However, this right can be derived from the reading together of Article 28(1) with the Articles 5 and 14(2) of the CRC. Article 5 contains the duty of the States to respect the rights and responsibilities of parents to provide guidance appropriate to the child's evolving capacities. Article 14(2) subjects the child's right to freedom of thought, conscience and religion to appropriate parental guidance. Hence, the States Parties to the CRC cannot overlook the religious and moral convictions of the parents in the education they offer. According to the CESCR Committee, this obligation means that public school instruction in subjects such as the general history of religions and ethics should be given in an unbiased and objective way, respectful of the freedoms of opinion, conscience and expression. Public education that includes instruction in a particular religion or belief is inconsistent with this right of the parents unless provision is made for non-discriminatory exemptions or alternatives that would accommodate the wishes of parents and guardians.[252] Also the European Court of Human Rights and the

---

[250] Traditionally, this right is expressly accorded to the parents: see Article 26(3) of the UDHR; Article 13(3) of the CESCR; Article 18(4) of the CCPR; Article 5(1)(b) of the UNESCO Convention against Discrimination in Education, Article 2 of the First Protocol to the ECHR and Article 13(4) of the Protocol San Salvador to the American Convention on Human Rights in the Area of Economic, Social and Cultural Rights.

Also during the draft of the CRC, there was a strong plea for the explicit inclusion of parental rights: *Travaux Préparatoires* (UN Docs. E/CN.4/1292, 1978, pp. 124–125; E/CN.4/1985/64, 1985, paras. 62 and 82; E/CN.4/1988/WG.1/WP.1/Rev.1, 1988, Article 15, para. 3; E/CN.4/1989/48, 1989, paras. 459 and 472), most of it reproduced in S. Detrick (ed.), *The United Nations Convention on the Rights of the Child: A Guide to the "Travaux Préparatoires"*, *o.c.* (note 88), pp. 384, 385, 391, 394. Eventually, this reference was considered as being superfluous as the rights and duties of the parents were dealt with elsewhere in the Convention: *Travaux Préparatoires* (UN Doc. E/CN.4/1989/48, 1989), paras. 462 and 472; reproduced in S. Detrick (ed.), *The United Nations Convention on the Rights of the Child: A Guide to the "Travaux Préparatoires"*, *o.c.* (note 88), pp. 392 and 394. The Holy See was concerned by this omission and made a reservation: UN Doc. CRC/C/2/Rev.8, 1999, p. 38.

[251] Explicitly guaranteed in Article 13(3) of the CESCR.

[252] CESCR Committee, *General Comment No. 13 on the Right to Education* (UN Doc. E/C.12/1999/10, 1999), para. 28.

Human Rights Committee are clear on this matter: respecting the parental religious and philosophical convictions entails that States must ensure an objective and pluralistic curriculum and abstain from indoctrinating pupils.[253]

Another parental right, which can be derived from Article 28(1), read together with Articles 5 and 29(2) of the CRC—and which is explicitly guaranteed in Article 13(3) of the CESCR—is the liberty of the parents to choose to send their children to other than public schools, provided that these schools conform to minimum standards laid down by the State. As Article 29(2) of the CRC guarantees the freedom of individuals and bodies to establish private schools, it is obvious that States Parties under the CRC should allow parents to send their children to these schools.

The difference with traditional human rights law,[254] however, is that the free choice of education is no longer an exclusive prerogative of the parents. The above mentioned implicit rights the parents have in the education of their children are subject to the underlying principles of the CRC, such as the best interest of the child[255] and the evolving capacities of the child.[256] Furthermore, the parental rights should be balanced against the child's own rights under the Convention, such as the right of the child to receive an education that promotes tolerance and respect of others[257] and its participation rights.[258] Also the right to privacy (Article 26 of the CRC) and to the non-discrimination principle (Article 2 of the CRC) are relevant in this context. According to the CRC Committee, the latter rights may be infringed by an education policy, which makes abstention from compulsory religious education dependent on the submission of a formal request exposing the faith of the child.[259] The Child's right to freedom of religion (Article

[253] Eur. Court HR, *Kjeldsen, Busk Madsen and Pedersen v. Denmark*, 7 December 1976, Series A, No. 23, para. 53 and Human Rights Committee, Communication No. 40/1978, *Hartikainen v. Finland*, 30 September 1978 (UN. Doc. CCPR/C/12/D/40/1978, 1978), para. 10.4.

[254] Although the European Court of Human Rights recognized that children should be protected against parental action that would violate their right to education (Eur. Court HR, *Kjeldsen, Busk Madsen and Pedersen v. Denmark*, 7 December 1976, Series A, No. 23, para. 52 and Eur. Court HR, *Martins Casimiro and Ferreira v. Luxemburg*, admissibility decision of 27 April 1999), it did not yet rule over the question whether children also have to be protected against parental action that does not threaten their right to education, which is for instance the case when a conflict arises between the religious and philosophical convictions of parents on the one hand and those of the child on the other hand.

[255] Article 3 CRC.

[256] Articles 5, 12(1) and 14(2) of the CRC.

[257] Article 29 of the CRC.

[258] In this context, especially Articles 12–14 of the CRC.

[259] *E.g.* CRC Committee, *Concluding Observations: Norway* (UN Doc. CRC/C/29, 1994), paras. 162 and 176.

14 of the CRC) should equally be taken into account in this context. The CRC Committee expressed its concern about a situation in which students require parental consent to attend ethics courses instead of religion courses.[260] Van Bueren points at a right of children to participate in decisions to help ensure that their education is in conformity with *their own* religious and moral convictions. A right, which can be derived from the combined reading of Articles 28(1), 5, 14(2) and 12.[261] Such an interpretation is in line with Article 5(1)(b) of the UNESCO Convention against Discrimination in Education, which states that no one should be compelled to receive religious instruction inconsistent with his or her conviction.[262] It may thus be concluded that the CRC foresees that children themselves also have a say in the choice of their education. Hence, in case of a conflict between the convictions of parents as far as religious education or school choice is concerned, the CRC requires a balanced approach between the rights of the parents on the one hand and those of their child on the other hand and prohibits an *a priori* exclusion of the position of the child.

37. Finally, a last aspect of the free choice of education should be mentioned, *i.e.* education in the language of one's choice. Article 28(1) does not refer to such a right. Also the jurisprudence of the European Court of Human Rights[263] reveals that there does not exist an obligation of States to organise education according to the linguistic preferences of the parents under the ECHR. The ECtHR only recognizes a right to be educated in the official language or one of the official languages of the State.[264] However, a tendency in the direction of a more flexible approach towards the right to education in a minority language can be deduced from the case *Cyprus v. Turkey*. The Court concluded that the Turkish-Cypriot authorities, which took the responsibility for the provision of Greek-language primary schooling, without continuing the provision of education in the Greek language at the secondary-school level, were denying the substance of the right to education of pupils belonging to the Greek minority. The option to continue secondary

---

[260] *E.g.* CRC Committee, *Concluding Observations: Poland* (UN Doc. CRC/C/15/Add.194, 2002), para. 33.

[261] G. Van Bueren, *The International Law on the Rights of the Child*, *o.c.* (note 18), p. 243. See also G. Van Bueren, 'Education: Whose Right is it Anyway' in: L. Hefferman (ed.), *Human Rights, A European perspective* (Dublin, Colour Books Ltd, The Round Hall Press and individual contributors, 1994), p. 346.

[262] The phrase does not only offer protection against State indoctrination, but can also serve as a basis for protecting children against religious instruction imposed by their parents.

[263] Herinafter referred to as ECtHR.

[264] ECtHR, *Belgian Linguistic Case*, 23 July 1978, Series A, No. 6, paras. 7 and 3.

education in the north was considered unrealistic in view of the fact that the children in question had already received their primary education in the Greek language. The other option of sending the children to a Greek-Cypriot school in the South was considered as too much a burden on their family life.[265] Without recognizing a general right to education in a minority language, the ECtHR thus stresses that if the State assumes responsibility for the organisation of education in a minority language, it should do it in such a way that the rights of the pupils and parents belonging to the minority group (in case the right to education at secondary level and the right to respect for family life) are not violated. Based on the contemporary human rights law on minority protection, Coomans also deduced a minimum obligation of the States not to frustrate the right of members of national, ethnic and linguistic minorities to be taught in their first language at institutions outside the official system of public education. This does however not entail an obligation of the States to subsidize these institutions.[266] Considering that the CRC protects children belonging to linguistic minorities to use their own language (Article 30 of the CRC), and that the CRC Committee recommended the organisation of multilingual education as an appropriate measure to fight the discrimination of minorities and indigenous populations in education (*cf. supra* No. 34), the holdings of the ECtHR as well as the conclusions of Coomans can be assumed to be guaranteed in Article 28(1) of the CRC.

38. It is also worth mentioning that international human rights law guarantees, next to the freedom to choose education, the freedom of individuals and bodies to establish and direct educational institutions. This liberty is neither explicitly nor implicitly enshrined in Article 28 of the CRC. It is entrenched in the second paragraph of the CRC's other main education provision, *i.e.* Article 29.[267] This sub-paragraph will not be commented upon in the present text as it is discussed in a separate volume of this CRC Commentary.

[265] ECtHR, *Cyprus v. Turkey*, 10 May 2001, Reports 2001–IV, para. 278.

[266] F. Coomans, 'In search of the core content of the right to education', *l.c.* (note 3), pp. 230–231.

[267] Also explicitly guaranteed in Article 13(4) of the CESCR and Article 13(5) of the Protocol San Salvador to the American Convention on Human Rights in the Area of Economic, Social and Cultural Rights.

1.4 *The Nature of States Parties' Obligations*

39. Article 28(1) imposes several clear obligations on the States Parties, of both a positive and a negative nature.

40. Most of the obligations enshrined in Article 28(1) are of a positive nature. These require a more active policy of the States and can be categorised in obligations 'to protect' and obligations 'to fulfil'.[268] Obligations 'to protect' require the States Parties to take measures that prevent third parties from interfering with the enjoyment of the right to education; *i.e.* guaranteeing the exercise of the right to education in horizontal relations. In this sense States must *inter alia* take measures to prevent and fight against discrimination in education organised by private educational institutions, and make sure that parents and employers do not stop children (especially girls) from going to school. Obligations 'to fulfil' require a variety of measures from the States in order to make the various types of education available and accessible for all and to maintain that level of realisation.[269] This category of obligations can further be subdivided in obligations 'to facilitate' and obligations 'to provide'. The obligation 'to facilitate' requires States to take positive measures that enable and assist individuals and communities to enjoy the right to education. Article 28(1) imposes the States for example to take positive measures to ensure substantive equality in education, to reduce school drop-outs and to prohibit child labour that interferes with the child's education. Finally, States Parties are obliged 'to provide' education. They have the primary responsibility for the direct provision of education at the level of primary, secondary and higher education.[270] They should among other things make sure that a system of schools is developed, which includes building classrooms, delivering programmes, providing teaching materials, training teachers and paying them domestically competitive salaries.[271] As has become clear above, the extent of the States' obligation to fulfil under Article 28(1) differs from level to level.

---

[268] CESCR Committee, *General Comment No. 13 on the Right to Education* (UN Doc. E/C.12/1999/10, 1999), para. 47. See also A. Eide, 'Economic, Social and Cultural Rights as Human Rights', in: A. Eide, C. Krause, A. Rosas (eds.), *Economic, Social and Cultural Rights* (Dordrecht/Boston/London, Martinus Nijhoff Publishers, 2001), pp. 23–24, and the Maastricht Guidelines on Violations of Economic, Social and Cultural Rights (UN Doc. E/C.12/2000/13, 2000), para. 6; reproduced in *Human Rights Quarterly* 20, 1998, pp. 691–705.

[269] F. Coomans, 'In search of the core content of the right to education', *l.c.* (note 3), p. 243.

[270] CESCR Committee, *General Comment No. 13 on the Right to Education* (UN Doc. E/C.12/1999/10, 1999), para. 48.

[271] *Ibid.*, para. 50.

41. These positive obligations may be fulfilled 'progressively' (Article 28(1) of the CRC) and 'to the maximum extent of their available resources' (Article 4 of the CRC).

Several notions used in Article 28(1) reveal the progressive nature of the States Parties' obligations. Firstly, the verb 'to recognize'—used in the *chapeau* of Article 28(1)—is closely linked with the idea of progressive realisation. This notion was during the drafting of Article 13(2) of the CESCR indeed explained as follows: 'recognition meant first and foremost that States should accept the obligation to do all in their power to achieve certain clearly defined aims, without, however, undertaking to attain them in a specified period. Admittedly, they could be achieved only by slow degrees, and the time involved would vary according to the relative magnitude of the problems of each country and the means at its disposal.'[272] Secondly, some argue that the verb 'to make'—which is used in several subparagraphs of Article 28(1)—reflects the progressive nature of the obligations.[273] Finally, the progressive nature of the obligations in Article 28(1) is once more reconfirmed by the sentence 'with a view to achieving this right progressively' in the *chapeau* of Article 28(1).

The inclusion of 'progressive realisation' constitutes a recognition of the fact that full realisation of the second generation rights will generally not be achieved in a short period of time because of a lack of financial and other resources.[274] However, this does not take away the fact that States have a clear obligation to fully realise the rights in the end. They should take steps within a reasonably short time after the CRC enters into force for them, in order to move towards this goal as expeditiously and effectively as possible.[275] Such steps must be deliberate, concrete and targeted towards the full realisation of the right to education.[276] 'Retrogressive' measures taken in

---

[272] UN Doc. E/CN.4/AC.14/SR.1, 1951.

[273] F. Coomans, 'In search of the core content of the right to education', *l.c.* (note 3), pp. 222, 224 and 236.

[274] CRC Committee, *General Comment No. 5: General measures of implementation of the Convention on the Rights of the Child* (UN Doc. CRC/GC/2003/5, 2003), para. 7; CESCR Committee, *General Comment No. 3 on the nature of States Parties obligations 1990* (UN Doc. HRI/GEN/1/Rev.5, 2001), para. 9.

[275] CESCR Committee, *General Comment No. 3 on the nature of States Parties obligations 1990* (UN Doc. HRI/GEN/1/Rev.5, 2001), paras. 2 and 9; and CESCR Committee, *General Comment No. 13 on the Right to Education* (UN Doc. E/C.12/1999/10, 1999), para. 44. See also the Limburg principles on the Implementation of the International Covenant on Economic, Social and Cultural Rights of 6 June 1986, *o.c.* (note 203), para. 21.

[276] CESCR Committee, *General Comment No. 3 on the nature of States Parties obligations 1990* (UN Doc. HRI/GEN/1/Rev.5, 2001), para. 2; and CESCR Committee, *General Comment No. 13 on the Right to Education* (UN Doc. E/C.12/1999/10, 1999), para. 43.

relation to education are, according to the CESCR Committee, presumed impermissible.[277] It can be assumed that also the CRC Committee considers retrogressive measures, such as a decrease in the education budget, as incompatible with the word 'progressively'.[278] As the term 'progressively' is mentioned in the *chapeau* of Article 28(1), States can fulfil their obligations under (a) till (e) in a progressive manner.

42. The second sentence of Article 4 of the CRC makes clear that the States should take steps 'to the maximum extent of their available resources'. The term 'resources' refers to both the resources existing within a State and those available from the international community through international cooperation and assistance.[279] The budgetary allocation for education is one of the focuses of the CRC Committee. In its reporting guidelines, the Committee asks the States to provide information on the proportion of the overall budget devoted to children and allocated to the various levels of education.[280] In its concluding observations to States Parties reports the Committee either welcomes an increase in the budget allocated to education,[281] or (and more commonly) is concerned about insufficient resource allocation to education[282] and therefore encourages States to ensure or raise budgetary allocations to education services.[283] The Committee remains, however, silent about what proportion of the national budget precisely should be allocated to education. The question as to when exactly the failure of a State to use the available resources to the maximum extent amounts to a

[277] CESCR Committee, *General Comment No. 3 on the nature of States Parties obligations 1990* (UN Doc. HRI/GEN/1/Rev.5, 2001), para. 9 and CESCR Committee, *General Comment No. 13 on the Right to Education* (UN Doc. E/C.12/1999/10, 1999), para. 45.

[278] R. Hodgkin and P. Newell, *o.c.* (note 79), p. 411.

[279] CESCR Committee, *General Comment No. 3 on the nature of States Parties obligations 1990* (UN Doc. HRI/GEN/1/Rev.5, 2001), para. 13. See also the Limburg principles on the Implementation of the International Covenant on Economic, Social and Cultural Rights of 6 June 1986, *o.c.* (note 203), para. 26.

[280] CRC Committee, *General Guidelines regarding the form and the contents of the periodic reports* (UN Doc. CRC/C/58, 1996), para. 106.

[281] *E.g.* CRC Committee, *Concluding Observations: Portugal* (UN Doc. CRC/C/46, 1995), para. 149; and *Yemen* (UN Doc. CRC/C/50, 1996), para. 51.

[282] *E.g.* CRC Committee, *Concluding Observations: Lebanon* (UN Doc. CRC/C/54, 1996), para. 36; *Zimbabwe* (UN Doc. CRC/C/54, 1996), para. 85; and *Nigeria* (UN Doc. CRC/C/50, 1996), para. 63.

[283] *E.g.* CRC Committee, *Concluding Observations: Yemen* (UN Doc. UN Doc. CRC/C/50, 1996), para. 45; *the former Federal Republic of Yugoslavia (Serbia and Montenegro)* (UN Doc. CRC/C/50, 1996), para. 108; *Zimbabwe* (UN Doc. CRC/C/54, 1996), para. 98; *Uruguay* (UN Doc. UN Doc. CRC/C/50, 1996), para. 117; *Burundi* (UN Doc. CRC/C/100, 2000), para. 104; *the Central African Republic* (UN Doc. CRC/C/100, 2000), para. 416; *Guinea-Bissau* (UN Doc. CRC/C/118, 2002), para. 75; *Eritrea* (UN Doc. CRC/C/132, 2003), para. 76; *Argentina* (UN Doc. CRC/C/121, 2002), para. 82; and *Pakistan* (UN Doc. CRC/C/133, 2004), para. 187.

breach of the Convention is therefore a difficult one to answer. All the more because the obligations to protect and to fulfil are obligations of result, leaving a large discretion to the State as to the means to accomplish these obligations.[284] The precise content of these obligations is therefore likely to vary from one State to another; and over time in relation to the same State.[285] Nevertheless, legal doctrine attempted to develop rules according to which a violation of internationally guaranteed education rights could be determined.[286] A concept that is often referred to in the determination of a violation of a socio-economic right is 'the minimum core content' of that right, to which 'minimum core obligations' correspond.[287] The notion 'minimum core content' refers to the essence and core substance of the right, which may not be violated by any State, including developing States. The notion 'to the maximum extent' should therefore in any case envelop the 'core content' of the right. As regards the identification of the 'core content' of the right to education enshrined in Article 28(1), reference can be made to the findings of Coomans with regard to the equivalent article in the CESCR.[288] In his opinion, the following elements of the right to education—corresponding to minimum positive obligations—constitute the minimum claims: Firstly, the right to enjoy free and compulsory primary education. Considering the fact that this right is an immediate obligation in the CESCR whilst a progressive one in the CRC (*cf. supra* No. 7, 14 and 17), the question arises whether Coomans' findings are transposable to the CRC. Bearing in mind

---

[284] A.P.M. Coomans, *De internationale bescherming van het recht op onderwijs, o.c.* (note 3), p. 124.

[285] P. Hunt, *State Obligations, indicators, benchmarks and the right to education* (UN Doc. E/C.12/1998/11, 1998), para. 6.

[286] See among others the Limburg principles on the Implementation of the International Covenant on Economic, Social and Cultural Rights of 6 June 1986, *o.c.* (note 203), paras. 70–73; the Maastricht Guidelines on Violations of Economic, Social and Cultural Rights, *o.c.* (note 268), paras. 6–32; A.R. Chapman, 'A "Violations Approach" for Monitoring the International Covenant on Economic, Social and Cultural Rights', *Human Rights Quarterly* 18, 1996, pp. 23–66; F. Coomans, 'In search of the core content of the right to education', *l.c.* (note 3), pp. 232–242; and V. Dankwa, C. Flinterman, and S. Leckie, 'Commentary to the Maastricht Guidelines on Violations of Economic, Social and Cultural Rights', *Human Rights Quarterly* 20, 1998, pp. 705–730.

[287] CESCR Committee, *General Comment No. 3 on the nature of States Parties obligations 1990* (UN Doc. HRI/GEN/1/Rev.5, 2001), para. 10; K. Arambulo, *Strengthening the Supervision of the International Covenant on Economic, Social and Cultural Rights, Theoretical and Procedural Aspects* (Antwerpen/Groningen/Oxford, Intersentia-Hart), 1999, pp. 130–136; A.P.M. Coomans, *De internationale bescherming van het recht op onderwijs, o.c.* (note 3), pp. 237–239; F. Coomans, 'In search of the core content of the right to education', *l.c.* (note 3), pp. 225–246; and M. Mehedi, *o.c.* (note 2), paras. 57–58.

[288] F. Coomans, 'In search of the core content of the right to education', *l.c.* (note 3), pp. 225–231.

the clarity of the text of Article 28(1)(a), the saving clause of Article 41 of the CRC (guaranteeing that the highest protection of the child will prevail), the importance given to these aspects by related international human rights treaties, the weight given to it by the CRC Committee as well as by other international monitoring bodies and its strong advocacy in legal doctrine, the obligation to make primary education cost-free and compulsory could be considered as constituting the core minimum obligations each State should fulfil in order to comply with Article 28(1) of the Convention. A second element of the core content of the right to education in Article 13 of the CESCR would be the right to special facilities for persons with an educational deficit or who would otherwise have no access to education at all, such as girls, children in rural areas, working children, street children, etc.[289] Article 28(1) clearly contains similar obligations (*cf. supra* No. 28–34). It is remarkable though that Coomans does not consider the category of refugees as falling within this group. He considers the promotion of education for refugees as a 'peripheral element' of the right to education, *i.e.* not belonging to the core.[290] In the light of Article 2 of the CRC, guaranteeing that the Convention applies to nationals and non-nationals alike and the Committee practice relating to education of refugee children (*cf. supra* No. 34), it is therefore more likely to conclude that the promotion of education for refugees under the CRC constitutes a core element. On the other hand, Coomans' opinion that promoting the instruction for indigenous children in their own language is a peripheral element can be transposed to the CRC context.[291] Although some obligations in this area can be derived from the text of the CRC (*cf. supra* No. 34 and 37), the Convention does not contain a general right for children belonging to a minority or an indigenous population to education in his or her own language. A third element identified as belonging to the core of the right to education and imposing positive obligations is the right to quality education at each educational level; also guaranteed in Article 28(1) (*cf. supra* No. 19). Van Bueren rightly identified a fourth core element of the right to education enshrined in Article 28(1), being the right of the child to be consulted on matters relating to his or her education, both at an individual level and at the level of policy making

[289] See also G. Van Bueren, 'The minimum core obligations of States under Article 10(3) of the International Covenant on Economic, Social and Cultural Rights', in: A. Chapman and S. Russell (eds.), *Core obligations: Building a Framework for Economic, Social and Cultural Rights* (Antwerp/Oxford/New York, Intersentia, 2002), pp. 150–153.

[290] F. Coomans, 'In search of the core content of the right to education', *l.c.* (note 3), p. 231.

[291] *Ibid.*, p. 231.

(*cf. infra* No. 45).[292] The corresponding obligations to these core elements of the right to education apply irrespective of the availability of resources and should thus also be fulfilled by developing countries.[293] Eide points out that a State claiming that it has not enough resources to fulfil even these core obligations has the burden of proving that this is due to reasons beyond its control and must prove that it has unsuccessfully sought to obtain international support.[294] The obligations of industrialised countries regarding education rights will exceed the 'core content' of these rights. These States may hence breach the CRC for not realising the, in Coomans' words, 'peripheral elements' of the right to education, such as providing different forms of secondary and higher education, setting up a system for educational and vocational information and guidance.[295]

43. Monitoring the States Parties' degree of compliance with progressive obligations 'to fulfil', can only be done if each State determines national benchmarks so as to increasingly fulfil more than the core obligations.[296] Also reliable and objective indicators should be developed. These may include literacy rates, public expenditure on education, enrolment ratios, completion and drop-out rates, book production etc.[297] A careful examination of these benchmarks and indicators over a period of several years followed by the identification of the root cause of a violation make it possible to indicate whether a State acted to the maximum extent of its available resources.[298]

---

[292] G. Van Bueren, 'The minimum core obligations of States under Article 10(3) of the International Covenant on Economic, Social and Cultural Rights', *l.c.* (note 289), p. 149.

[293] The Maastricht Guidelines on Violations of Economic, Social and Cultural Rights, *o.c.* (note 268), paras. 9–10.

[294] A. Eide, 'Economic, Social and Cultural Rights as Human Rights', *l.c.* (note 268), p. 27.

[295] F. Coomans, 'In search of the core content of the right to education', *l.c.* (note 3), p. 231.

[296] P. Hunt, *o.c.* (note 285), paras. 13–23; K. Tomaševski, *Annual Report of the Special Rapporteur on the Right to Education 2001/29* (UN Doc. E/CN.4/2002/60, 2002), paras. 30–37; and K. Tomaševski, *Annual Report of the Special Rapporteur on the Right to Education 2002/23* (UN Doc. E/CN.4/2003/9, 2003), paras. 26–28.

[297] M. Nowak, 'The right to education—Its meaning, significance and limitations', *l.c.* (note 49), p. 424. On indicators, measuring the realisation and violation of the right to education, see among others K. Beeckman, 'Measuring the implementation of the right to education', *The International Journal of Children's Rights* 12, No, 2004, pp. 71–84; K. Halvorsen, 'Notes on the Realization of the Human Right to Education', *l.c.* (note 114), pp. 357–362, P. Hunt, *o.c.* (note 285), paras. 9–12; K. Tomaševski, 'Indicators', in A. Eide et al. (eds.), *Economic, Social and Cultural Rights*, Dordrecht/Boston/London, Martinus Nijhoff Publishers, 2001, pp. 531–543 and K. Tomaševski, *Annual Report of the Special Rapporteur on the Right to Education 2001/29*, (UN Doc. E/CN.4/2002/60, 2002), paras. 27–45. Also the CRC Committee insists in its reporting guidelines on the development of appropriate indicators: see CRC Committee, *General Guidelines regarding the form and the contents of the periodic reports* (UN Doc. CRC/C/58, 1996), paras. 18 and 20 and (UN Doc. CRC/C/57, 1996), para. 222.

[298] M. Nowak, 'The Right to Education', *l.c.* (note 3), pp. 256–257.

44. Although the phrases 'to recognize' and 'with a view to achieve this right progressively' are part of the *chapeau* of Article 28(1), not all obligations enshrined in this paragraph are of a progressive nature. Some should be realised immediately by all States Parties, whatever their stage of economic development. These are the so-called obligations 'to respect'. An obligation 'to respect' requires States Parties to avoid measures that hinder or prevent the enjoyment of the right to education.[299] They have a negative meaning, that is, a prohibition against State interference. States have, for example, under Article 28(1) the immediate obligation to respect the equality principle in public schools and the obligation to respect the child's and the parents' choice of religious education and type of school. Violations of these immediate obligations can much more easily be traced as they can be seen as an obligation of conduct:[300] if a State Party did not follow the course of action specified in Article 28(1) within a reasonably short period after the CRC entered into force for that State, it is clearly in breach with the Convention. This is confirmed by the fact that the obligations 'to respect' have been identified as belonging to the 'core content' of the right to education,[301] and thus should be realised regardless the economic context of a State.

1.5 *The Right-holders—Child Participation in Education*

45. Article 28(1) explicitly refers to 'the child' as holder of the right to education. In terms of Article 1 of the CRC, a child means 'every human being below the age of 18 years unless, under the law applicable to the child, majority is attained earlier'. Though an explicit reference is inherent to an instrument that was expressly drafted to guarantee the rights of the child, this phenomenon is extraordinary in international human rights law on education, which traditionally accords this right to 'everyone'. Although the latter notion also includes children as beneficiaries of the education rights, the child's own rights were traditionally overshadowed by the rights

---

[299] CESCR Committee, *General Comment No. 13 on the Right to Education* (UN Doc. E/C.12/1999/10, 1999), para. 47.

[300] F. Coomans, 'In search of the core content of the right to education', *l.c.* (note 3), p. 243.

[301] More precisely, Coomans identified the right to equal access to the existing public educational institutions, the right to the same quality of education for all, and the free choice of education without coercion by the State with respect to religious and philosophical convictions and language of instruction as being the main claims under Article 13 of the CESCR, which can be assumed as equally constituting the core 'negative' obligations under Article 28(1) of the CRC: F. Coomans, 'In search of the core content of the right to education', *l.c.* (note 3), pp. 225–231.

and duties the parents have with regard to the education of their child.[302] Article 28(1) gives way to a more balanced approach to education as belonging to children as well as to parents, especially with regard to some traditional parental rights in education. As has already been pointed out above (*cf. supra* No. 36), the issue of the free choice of education is no longer an exclusive prerogative of the parents. The CRC guarantees that the convictions of both, the parents and the child should be taken into account in the choice of the kind of education. In case of a conflict between the convictions of parents on the one hand and those of their child on the other hand, *a priori* exclusion of the position of the child, would constitute a violation of the CRC. Also other educational matters, such as the content of the curriculum, exam schedules, pedagogic style, school facilities (toilets, pupil lockers, vending machines etc.) sports events, dressing code etc. should be approached from a more child-participatory perspective. This becomes apparent from the reading together of Article 28 and the CRC's participation provisions,[303] yielding to the obligations of States Parties to give sufficient attention to the right of the child to express his/her view in educational matters. The CRC Committee is of the opinion that children should be systematically involved in education matters, such as sex education programmes at school and exclusion from school. Neither the parents nor the school management may decide without hearing the child's opinion.[304] In order to ensure participation in school policy, governments should make sure that schools are in the possibility to introduce some appropriate and structural[305] institutional mechanisms. What kind of structures and mechanisms States Parties should establish precisely, mainly remains an open question. Some indications can however be found in the recommendations made by the CRC Committee and by some authors. In the first place, the Committee recommends to incorporate the participation articles of the CRC into domestic education laws and procedures.[306] The inclusion in legislation is however only the first step. In the second place this legislation should be implemented. The Committee therefore recommends the effective introduction

---

[302] G. Van Bueren, *The International Law on the Rights of the Child, o.c.* (note 18), p. 232; See also G. Van Bueren, 'Education: Whose Right is it Anyway' *l.c.* (note 261), p. 339.

[303] Especially Articles 12, 13, 14, and 15 of the CRC.

[304] *E.g.* CRC Committee, *Concluding Observations: the United Kingdom of Great-Britain and Northern Ireland* (UN Doc. CRC/C/38, 1995), para. 218; and *Belgium* (UN Doc. CRC/C/43, 1995), para. 111.

[305] *I.e.* no short-term projects: G. Lansdown, *Promoting children's participation in democratic decision-making* (Italy, Unicef Innocenti Research Centre, 2001), p. 12.

[306] *E.g.* CRC Committee, *Concluding Observations: Armenia* (UN Doc. CRC/C/15/Add.119), para. 26.

of procedures to ensure that children are provided with the opportunity to express their views on the running of the schools in matters concerning them and that due weight is given to these opinions.[307] With regard to expulsion from school, for instance, it is suggested that a child should have the right to appeal against this decision.[308] In the third place, some scholars point out that the governments should provide the partners in play with the necessary support. Implementation of participation rights requires that both children as well as adults should be informed about human rights, including participation. Firstly, children themselves should be equipped with skills to participate, such as advocacy, counselling and listening skills.[309] The CRC Committee recommends the States therefore to provide for quality counselling programmes in schools.[310] Secondly, those who live and work with children (parents, teachers, other care-givers) should be sufficiently trained in genuine participation.[311] The parents and the wider community indeed have a great role to play in the realisation of a child's participation rights. They should create the opportunities for children to participate; they should give appropriate direction, guidance or advice to the child so that it increasingly assumes responsibilities, becomes active, tolerant and democratic, without being manipulative.[312] In this way an appropriate climate for participation at school can be created. The CRC Committee therefore recommends to provide educational information to among others parents, teachers and society at large on children's participation rights.[313]

---

[307] *E.g.* CRC Committee, *Concluding Observations: the United Kingdom of Great-Britain and Northern Ireland* (UN Doc. CRC/C/38, 1995), para. 234; *Nigeria* (UN Doc. CRC/C/50, 1996), para. 91; *Venezuela* (UN Doc. CRC/C/90, 1999), para. 46; *the United Kingdom of Great Britain and Northern Ireland—Isle of Man* (UN Doc. CRC/C/100, 2000), para. 199; *Finland* (UN Doc. CRC/C/100, 2000), paras. 55–56; *Belgium* (UN Doc. CRC/C/118, 2002), para. 113; and *the United Kingdom of Great Britain and Northern Ireland* (UN Doc. CRC/C/121, 2002), paras.122 and 140.

[308] *E.g.* CRC Committee, *Concluding Observations: the United Kingdom of Great-Britain and Northern Ireland* (UN Doc. CRC/C/38, 1995), para. 234; and *the United Kingdom of Great Britain and Northern Ireland* (UN Doc. CRC/C/121, 2002), para. 140.

[309] A. Osler and H. Starkey, 'Children's rights and citizenship: some implications for the management of schools', *The International Journal of Children's Rights* 6, 1998, p. 326; and S. De Groof and M. Elchardus, *Leerlingenparticipatie nader bekeken [A closer look at participation of pupils]* (Brussels, Ministerie van de Vlaamse Gemeenschap, 2003), p. 3.

[310] *E.g.* CRC Committee, *Concluding Observations: New Zealand* (UN Doc. CRC/C/133, 2004), para. 156.

[311] *E.g.* CRC Committee, *Concluding Observations: India* (UN Doc. CRC/C/15/Add.115, 2000), paras. 34–35; G. Lansdown, *o.c.* (note 305), p. 2; M. Santos Pais, 'Child Participation', *Documentação e Direito Comparado* 81/82, 2000, p. 96; and R. Hodgkin and P. Newell, *o.c.* (note 79), p. 168.

[312] B. Franklin, 'Children's Right to Participate in Decision Making. A case study of Ravenswood Primary School Council Newcastle upon Tyne, England', in: E. Verhellen, *Monitoring Children's Rights* (The Hague, Martinus Nijhoff Publishers), 1996, p. 323.

[313] *E.g.* CRC Committee, *Concluding Observations: the Dominican Republic* (UN Doc. CRC/C/15/Add.

2. *Article 28(2): The Right to a Humane Disciplinary System*

46. The second paragraph of Article 28 of the CRC constitutes the first treaty standard, which expressly obliges the States Parties in the framework of education rights to take 'all appropriate measures to ensure that school discipline is administered in a manner consistent with the child's human dignity and in conformity with the present Convention.' It guarantees—together with the requirements regarding the content of education (*cf. supra* No. 19)—that education is 'acceptable' to the child.

47. In the first place, this sub-article aims at the protection of children against an *inhuman or degrading* disciplinary system at school. The words 'in conformity with the present Convention' refer in this sense mainly to the Articles 19 and 37(a) of the CRC.[314] Article 19 protects children from all forms of physical and mental maltreatment perpetrated by parents, legal guardians or any other person who has the care of the child. The CRC Committee confirmed the applicability of this article to schools and other educational institutions.[315] It follows that the phrase 'any other person who has the care of the child' includes teachers and other personnel in schools. Article 37(a) guarantees the prohibition of torture or other cruel, inhuman or degrading treatment or punishment.

The concluding observations of the CRC Committee reveal that both excessive and moderate forms of corporal punishment are unacceptable and incompatible with the Articles 28(2), 19, 37(a) and even 29[316] of the CRC. Not only corporal punishment but also any other treatment which is cruel, inhuman or degrading, such as bullying and verbal aggression,[317] or public humiliation[318] constitute an infringement of the rights enshrined in the CRC. States

150, 2001), para. 25; *Nicaragua* (UN Doc. CRC/C/15/Add.108, 1999), para. 25; *Liberia* (UN Doc. CRC/C/15/Add.236, 2004), para. 29; *Madagascar* (UN Doc. CRC/C/133, 2004), para. 284; and *Panama* (UN Doc. CRC/C/15/Add.233, 2004), para. 28. See also CRC Committee, *General Guidelines regarding the form and the contents of the periodic reports* (UN Doc. CRC/C/58, 1996), para. 46.

[314] S. Detrick, *A Commentary on the United Nations Convention on the Rights of the Child, o.c* (note 101), p. 489.

[315] *E.g.* CRC Committee, *Concluding Observations: Bolivia* (UN Doc. CRC/C/80, 1998), para. 108.

[316] CRC Committee, *General Comment No. 1 on the Aims of Education* (UN Doc. CRC/GC/2001/1, 2001), para. 8.

[317] CRC Committee, *General Discussion Day on violence against children in the family and at school* (UN Doc. CRC/C/111, 2001), paras. 679, 696 and 706. See also CRC Committee, *Concluding Observations: Korea* (UN Doc. CRC/C/50, 1996), para. 171; *Zimbabwe* (UN Doc. CRC/C/54, 1996), para. 101; and *Tunisia* (UN Doc. CRC/C/118, 2002), para. 290.

[318] CESCR Committee, *General Comment No. 13 on the Right to Education* (UN Doc. E/C.12/1999/10, 1999), para. 41.

must adopt measures in order to prohibit such actions *de jure* and *de facto*. The Committee therefore encouraged States to take legal measures to prohibit physical punishment.[319] States are also encouraged to take repressive measures, such as punishing the perpetrator and reporting incidents of corporal punishment through the establishment of child-sensitive structures for complaints. Also preventative measures are encouraged, such as the setting up of awareness raising campaigns regarding the negative consequences of corporal punishment as well as the promotion of alternative measures.[320]

The general prohibition of torture, inhuman and degrading treatment is enshrined in several human rights instruments.[321] The holdings of the CRC Committee regarding corporal punishment are therefore in line with the findings of other international and regional monitoring bodies. The Human Rights Committee maintained that corporal punishment is in breach with the prohibition of torture under Article 7 of the CCPR.[322] Also the ECtHR recognized the inconsistency of corporal punishment at school with the prohibition of torture, inhuman and degrading treatment (Article 3 ECHR). The Court held that the minimum standard of degrading treatment within the meaning of Article 3 of the ECHR can be reached in cases of corporal punishment in school settings. In *Campbell and Cosans* the disciplinary measure, constituting the use of a leather strap to strike the palm of the hand,

---

[319] *E.g.* CRC Committee, *Concluding Observations: the United Kingdom of Great-Britain and Northern Ireland* (UN Doc. CRC/C/38, 1995), paras. 218 and 233–234; *Korea* (UN Doc. CRC/C/50, 1996), para. 171; *Zimbabwe* (UN Doc. UN Doc. CRC/C/54, 1996), para. 101; *the United Kingdom of Great-Britain and Northern Ireland—Isle of Man* (UN Doc. CRC/C/100, 2000), paras. 90–91; *the Democratic Republic of the Congo* (UN Doc. CRC/C/108, 2001), para. 188; *the United Arabic Emirates* (UN Doc. CRC/C/118, 2002), para. 401; *Tunisia* (UN Doc. CRC/C/118, 2002), para. 290; *Argentina* (UN Doc. CRC/C/121, 2002), para. 64; *India* (UN Doc. CRC/C/15/Add.228, 2004), para. 45; *Indonesia* (UN Doc. CRC/C/15/Add.223, 2004), para. 44; and *France* (UN Doc. CRC/C/14/Add.240, 2004), para. 39.

[320] *E.g.* CRC Committee, *Concluding Observations: Belize* (UN Doc. CRC/C/84, 1999), para. 78; *Luxemburg* (UN Doc. CRC/C/79, 1998), para. 272; *Guinea* (UN Doc. CRC/C/84, 1999), para. 110; *Thailand* (UN Doc. CRC/C/80, 1998), para. 172; *Kuwait* (UN Doc. CRC/C/80, 1998), para. 139; *Tajikistan* (UN Doc. CRC/C/100, 2000), para. 302; *the Democratic Republic of the Congo* (UN Doc. CRC/C/108, 2001), para. 188; *Oman* (UN Doc. CRC/C/111, 2001), paras. 195–196; *Cameroon* (UN Doc. CRC/C/111, 2001), para. 380; *St. Vincent and the Grenadines* (UN Doc. CRC/C/118, 2002), para. 440; *Zambia* (UN Doc. CRC/C/132, 2003), para. 208; *Belgium* (UN Doc. CRC/C/15/Add. 178, 2002), para. 24; *Tunisia* (UN Doc. CRC/C/118, 2002), para. 290; *Argentina* (UN Doc. CRC/C/121, 2002), para. 64; *India* (UN Doc. CRC/C/15/Add.228, 2004), para. 45; *Indonesia* (UN Doc. CRC/C/15/Add.223, 2004), para. 44; *Panama* (UN Doc. CRC/C/15/Add.233, 2004), para. 34. See also CRC Committee, *Day of General Discussion on violence against children in the family and at school* (UN Doc. CRC/C/111, 2001), paras. 714–732.

[321] See among others Article 7 of the CCPR, Article 3 of the ECHR and Article 37 of the CRC.

[322] Human Rights Committee, *General Comment No. 20: Prohibition of torture and cruel treatment or punishment (Art.7)* (UN Doc. HRI/GEN/1/Rev.5, 1992), p. 139, para. 5.

was not considered to be a violation, only because the punishment was actually not executed. The mere risk to get strapped was in this case not considered as severe enough to be qualified as degrading treatment.[323] In the case *Warwick*, where the corporal punishment in fact had been carried out, the Commission found a violation of Article 3.[324] Article 3 ECHR can thus only be violated if the punishment has been executed. Article 2 of Protocol No. 1 to the ECHR, on the other hand, can be infringed by the mere existence of a system of corporal punishment at school, which is in line with Article 28(2) of the CRC. In the case *Campbell and Cosans*, the ECtHR recognized that a disciplinary system, including corporal punishment may violate the right of the parents to have their philosophical convictions respected in the education of their children (second sentence of Article 2 of Protocol No. 1 to the ECHR).[325] Also the pupil's suspension from school, due to his parents refusal to accept the existence of corporal punishment as a disciplinary matter, was considered as a denial of his right to education (first sentence of Article 2 of Protocol No. 1 to the ECHR).[326]

48. Disciplinary measures at school should not only be consistent with the prohibition of torture, inhuman and degrading treatment; they also must be in conformity with *the other human rights of children and their human dignity*.[327] This requirement is innovative in international law. In this sense, schools may not impose measures, which would impede the contact with the parents, which would interfere with the child's participation to his or her culture or use of his or her language, which would disproportionately hinder the exercise of the participation rights and their right to rest and leisure or which would breach the child's right to food.[328] Moreover, disciplinary measures should be in conformity with the general principles, such as the best interest principle, and the non-discrimination principle.[329] With

---

[323] ECtHR, *Campbell and Cosans v. the United Kingdom*, 25 February 1982, Series A, No. 48, paras. 24–31.

[324] ECmHR, No. 9471/81, *Warwick v. the United Kingdom*, Comm. Rep., 18 July 1986, *D.R.* 60, pp. 5–24.

[325] ECtHR, *Campbell and Cosans v. the United Kingdom*, 25 February 1982, Series A, No. 48, paras. 32–38.

[326] *Ibid.*, paras. 40–41.

[327] G. Van Bueren, *The International Law on the Rights of the Child, o.c.* (note 18), p. 249; Also the UNESCO against Discrimination in Education proscribes practices in education which are an infringement of human dignity (see Article 1).

[328] R. Hodgkin and P. Newell, *o.c.* (note 79), p. 425. Regarding the compatibility of the disciplinary system with the right to food, see also CESCR Committee, *General Comment No. 13 on the Right to Education* (UN Doc. E/C.12/1999/10, 1999), para. 41.

[329] CRC Committee, *General Guidelines regarding the form and the contents of the periodic reports* (UN Doc. CRC/C/58, 1996), para. 109.

regard to non-discrimination, much emphasis has been put by the CRC Committee as well as by the Special Rapporteur on the right to education on the elimination of the interpretation of pregnancy as a disciplinary offence (*cf. supra* No. 26). The CRC Committee also has devoted much attention to child participation in disciplinary procedures. The child should be able to express its views when a disciplinary measure, such as decision of expulsion of the child is under consideration (Article 12(1) of the CRC). Furthermore, children should be heard in all judicial and administrative proceedings regarding their education, including disciplinary proceedings (Article 12(2) of the CRC). This means in the first place that schools may not impose measures, which would hinder the exercise of the participation rights.[330] In the second place, some positive measures will be needed to fulfil genuine participation (*cf. supra* No. 45). The CRC Committee expressly asks States to report on the adopted legislation providing the opportunity for the child to participate in administrative proceedings relating to disciplinary measures, such as school exclusion,[331] and encourages States to do so in its concluding observations.[332] Moreover, the Committee recommends States to launch awareness raising campaigns for the introduction of disciplinary measures, which comply with the human rights of children.[333]

49. The CRC Committee recognised the horizontal effect of Article 28(2). In its reporting guidelines, it asks the States to adopt legislative measures in order to proscribe corporal punishment and other forms of disciplinary measures that infringe the rights of the child in private schools.[334] In its concluding observations it urged States to introduce legislation banning the use of corporal punishment in private schools.[335] The obligations enshrined in it hence should be respected in both public and private educational institutions. The view of the CRC Committee can be confirmed by reference to the viewpoints of the European Commission and Court of Human Rights in

---

[330] R. Hodgkin and P. Newell, *o.c.* (note 79), p. 426.

[331] CRC Committee, *General Guidelines regarding the form and the contents of the periodic reports* (UN Doc. CRC/C/58, 1996), para. 109.

[332] *E.g.* CRC Committee, *Concluding Observations: Suriname* (UN Doc. CRC/C/97, 2000), para. 500.

[333] *E.g.* CRC Committee, *Concluding Observations: the United Kingdom of Great-Britain and Northern Ireland* (UN Doc. CRC/C/38, 1995), para. 218; *Thailand* (UN Doc. CRC/C/80, 1998), para. 172; *Ireland* (UN Doc. CRC/C/73, 1998), para. 101; *Japan* (UN Doc. CRC/C/79, 1998), para. 191; and *Kuwait* (UN Doc. CRC/C/80, 1998), para. 139.

[334] CRC Committee, *General Guidelines regarding the form and the contents of the periodic reports* (UN Doc. CRC/C/58, 1996), para. 109.

[335] *E.g.* CRC Committee, *Concluding Observations: the United Kingdom* (UN Doc. CRC/C/15/Add.34, 1995), para. 16.

this regard.[336] In the case *Y.*, the Commission found that a headmaster in a private school, caning a pupil four times through his trousers, constituted degrading treatment within the meaning of Article 3 ECHR.[337] In another case regarding corporal punishment in a private school, *i.e. Costello-Roberts*, the Commission decided, however, that giving three 'whacks' with a gym shoe on the bottom of a seven-year-old boy could not be considered as severe enough to constitute degrading treatment. A violation was, however, found of the pupil's right to respect his private life under Article 8 ECHR.[338] Although the Court did not find a violation neither of Article 3 nor of Article 8, it recognised the State responsibility for disciplinary measures in private schools.[339] The view of the European Convention organs validates the observations of the CRC Committee. Also the CESCR Committee stressed the horizontal effect of the right to a humane disciplinary system at school.[340]

50. As becomes apparent from the above, Article 28(2) imposes both negative and positive obligations on the States Parties. Firstly, States have some obligations of a negative and thus immediate character. In this sense, States have for instance the immediate obligation not to infringe upon a child's human rights and dignity whilst imposing disciplinary measures in State-run schools. Secondly, States have positive obligations under this sub-paragraph. They should *inter alia* protect children against an inhumane disciplinary system in private schools and should take positive measures in order to ensure that for instance participation rights are respected in disciplinary systems in both public and private schools.

3. *Article 28(3): International Cooperation in Education*

51. According to Article 28(3) 'States Parties shall promote and encourage international cooperation in matters relating to education, in particular with a view to contributing to the elimination of ignorance and illiteracy throughout the world and facilitating access to scientific and technical

---

336 M. Nowak, 'The Right to Education', *l.c.* (note 3), p. 265; see also U. Kilkelly, *The Child and the European Convention on Human Rights* (Aldershot, Ashgate/Dartmouth, 1999), pp. 167–168.

337 ECmHR, No. 14229/88, *Y v. the United Kingdom*, Comm. Rep., 8 oktober 1991. The case did not appear before the Court because a friendly settlement was reached.

338 ECmHR, No. 13134/87, *Costello-Roberts v. the United Kingdom*, Comm. Rep., 8 June 1991.

339 ECtHR, *Costello-Roberts v. the United Kingdom*, 25 March 1993, *Publ. Hof*, Serie A, No. 247–C, paras. 26–28.

340 CESCR Committee, *General Comment No. 13 on the Right to Education* (UN Doc. E/C.12/1999/10, 1999), para. 41.

knowledge and modern teaching methods. In this regard, particular account shall be taken of the needs of developing countries.' This paragraph is a specification of the provision in Article 4, which pleads for the stimulation of international cooperation in order to improve the realisation of social, economic and cultural rights.[341] It is the most comprehensive call in a binding human rights instrument addressed to the States Parties to co-operate internationally in educational matters. Other references to the necessity of international co-operation in the effective realisation of the right to education can be found in Articles 2, 23 and 15(4) of the CESCR, Articles 55 and 56 of the Charter of the United Nations, Article 10 of the World Declaration on Education for All,[342] Articles 10–14 and 21 of the Dakar Framework for Action,[343] as well as in some other UNESCO instruments,[344] and in the 1993 Vienna Declaration and Programme of Action.[345]

52. In Article 28(3), the right to education is approached as a third generation right:[346] in the framework of the right to education, the beneficiaries in developing countries have a right to solidarity. According to some authors this implies a corresponding duty to solidarity for the industrialised countries.[347] The latter should fulfil this obligation by means of appropriate legislation, institution building and policy.[348] It is indeed difficult not to draw any obligation for the industrialised countries from the words of Article 28(3), backed by the wordings of Article 4 and the preamble of the Convention.[349] All the more because the holdings of both the CRC

[341] Similar specifications can be found in the 23(4) and 24(4) of the CRC.

[342] World Declaration on Education for All, adopted in 1990 in Jomtien (Thailand), *o.c.* (note 42), p. 77.

[343] Dakar Framework for Action, adopted in 2000 in Dakar (Senegal), *o.c.* (note 42), pp. 9–10.

[344] See Article 1.2.(c) of the UNESCO Constitution and among others Articles 43–45 of the Education Recommendation concerning education for international understanding, co-operation and peace and education relating to human rights and fundamental freedoms, adopted on 19 November 1974.

[345] World Conference on Human Rights: Vienna Declaration and Programme of Action (UN Doc. A/CONF.157/23, 1993), para. 34.

[346] M. Nowak, 'The Right to Education', *l.c.* (note 3), pp. 254–255; M. Mehedi, *o.c.* (note 2), para. 51.

[347] See among others M. Bedjaoui in: H.J. Steiner and Ph. Alston, *International Human Rights in Context* (Oxford, University Press, 2000), p. 1323 and M. Nowak, 'The Right to Education', *l.c.* (note 3), pp. 254–255.

[348] Bedjaoui makes a similar reasoning as regards the right to development: see M. Bedjaoui, *l.c.* (note 347), p. 1323.

[349] The preamble of the CRC states: '. . . Recognizing the importance of international cooperation for improving the living conditions of children in every country, in particular in the developing countries'.

Committee[350] and the CESCR Committee[351] point in this direction. The CRC Committee maintains that 'when States ratify the Convention, they take upon themselves obligations not only to implement it within their jurisdiction, but also to contribute, through international cooperation, to global implementation'.[352] The CESCR Committee stresses that particularly those States which are in a position to assist others should fulfil the obligation reflected in Articles 55 and 56 of the UN Charter to international cooperation for development and thus for the realisation of economic, social and cultural rights.[353] The developed countries would have this obligation both individually and as members of international organizations, including international financial institutions.[354] However, the views of others reflect the necessity to interpret this article in a more cautious way. Alston and Quinn point out that, the *Travaux Préparatoires* of the CESCR reveal disagreement as to the question whether the similar provisions in the CESCR entail a duty for industrialised countries.[355] The consensus as to whether Article 28(3) entails an obligation for the industrialised States to international cooperation is therefore still to be found.

Less controversial is the question whether Article 28(3) entails an obligation of the developing countries to search for international assistance. The reading together of the Articles 28(3) and 4 reflects such an obligation. Article 4 indeed obliges the States to undertake implementation measures to the maximum extent of their available resources and, 'where needed,

---

[350] CRC Committee, *General Comment No. 5: General measures of implementation of the Convention on the Rights of the Child* (UN Doc. CRC/GC/2003/5, 2003), paras. 7, 60–64. See also CRC Committee, *General Guidelines regarding the form and the contents of the periodic reports* (UN Doc. CRC/C/58, 1996), para. 111.

[351] CESCR Committee, *General Comment No. 3 on the nature of States Parties obligations 1990* (UN Doc. HRI/GEN/1/Rev.5, 2001), paras. 13 and 14 and CESCR Committee, *General Comment No. 13 on the Right to Education* (UN Doc. E/C.12/1999/10, 1999), para. 56.

[352] CRC Committee, *General Comment No. 5: General measures of implementation of the Convention on the Rights of the Child* (UN Doc. CRC/GC/2003/5, 2003), para. 7.

[353] CESCR Committee, *General Comment No. 3 on the nature of States Parties obligations 1990* (UN Doc. HRI/GEN/1/Rev.5, 2001), para. 14.

[354] CRC Committee, *General Comment No. 5: General measures of implementation of the Convention on the Rights of the Child* (UN Doc. CRC/GC/2003/5, 2003), paras. 63–64; and CESCR Committee, *General Comment No. 13 on the Right to Education* (UN Doc. E/C.12/1999/10, 1999), para. 60.

[355] The authors do not exclude a binding obligation for the industrialised countries but stay vague in their statements: 'In the context of a given right it may, accordingly to the circumstances, be possible to identify obligations to cooperate internationally that would appear to be mandatory on the basis of the undertaking contained in Article 2(1) of the Covenant': Ph. Alston and G. Quinn, 'The Nature and Scope of States' Parties' Obligations under the International Covenant on Economic, Social and Cultural Rights', *Human Rights Quarterly* 9, 1987, p. 191; reproduced in H.J. Steiner and Ph. Alston, *International Human Rights in Context* (Oxford, Oxford University Press, 2000), p. 1328.

within the framework of international co-operation'. The CRC Committee stresses the importance to look for international assistance in order to realise the right to education,[356] and states that governments 'need to be able to demonstrate that they, when necessary, have sought international cooperation'.[357]

53. Article 28(3) is silent about the type and extent of the assistance. It is clear that the international cooperative actions should relate to 'matters relating to education'. The meaning of the notion 'education' in this sub-paragraph may be considered in the same broad sense of the notion in sub-paragraph 28(1) (*cf. supra* No. 9). The phrases 'the elimination of ignorance and illiteracy' and 'facilitating access to scientific and technical knowledge', imply an activity which goes beyond mere instruction at school. Technical aid and assistance thus should relate to both a) the provision of basic skills, and b) the development of the intellectual, spiritual, and emotional potential of the young person or in other words the broader development of his or her personality and comprising both formal and non-formal educational systems. The CRC Committee gave some more concrete indications as to the type of assistance. In the framework of its competence under Article 45(b) of the CRC,[358] the Committee identified a need for technical advice and assistance and consequently referred reports,[359] especially to UNICEF and UNESCO. Frequently the call was phrased in general wordings, such as 'international assistance in the area of education' or 'cooperation to strengthen the educational system and policy'. But often also more specific aid was asked for in order to achieve specific aims such as listed below,

- to conduct training programmes on human rights for professionals working with and for children;
- to include human rights subjects in the school curricula;
- to increase the quality and relevance of education;

[356] *E.g.* CRC Committee, *Concluding Observations: Jordan* (UN Doc. CRC/C/97, 2000), para. 200; *Côte d'Ivoire* (UN Doc. CRC/C/108, 2001), para. 338; *Kenya* (UN Doc. CRC/C/111, 2001), para. 135; *Cameroon* (UN Doc. CRC/C/111, 2001), para. 380; *Gambia* (UN Doc. CRC/C/111, 2001), para. 453; *Guinea-Bissau* (UN Doc. CRC/C/118, 2002), para. 75. See also CRC Committee, *General Guidelines regarding the form and the contents of the periodic reports* (UN Doc. CRC/C/58, 1996), para. 111.

[357] CRC Committee, *General Comment No. 5: General measures of implementation of the Convention on the Rights of the Child* (UN Doc. CRC/GC/2003/5, 2003), para. 7.

[358] Under this Article the CRC Committee has the competence to send reports that contain a request or show a need for technical support to specialised agencies, UNICEF and other competent bodies.

[359] *E.g.* UN Docs. CRC/C/40/Rev. 18, 2001 and CRC/C/40/Rev. 21, 2002.

- to ensure access to education for the most vulnerable groups;
- to increase the numbers of schools and classes available;
- to train more teachers and school inspectors;
- to develop the standard national textbooks;
- to raise rates of enrolment;
- to provide assistance with school fees, uniforms and other equipment to poor families.

Specific actions and strategies to be developed by the donor and creditor countries in order to achieve these aims can be found in Article 11 of the Dakar Framework for Action. They include increasing external finance for education, ensuring greater predictability in the flow of external assistance, facilitating more effective donor co-ordination, undertaking more effective and regular monitoring of progress, and providing earlier, more extensive and broader debt relief and/or debt cancellation for poverty reduction, with strong commitment to basic education.[360] The latter has also been advocated by the CRC Committee,[361] the Special Rapporteur on the right to education,[362] and by the Secretary General of the United Nations.[363]

The phrase 'In this regard, particular account shall be taken of the needs of developing countries' indicates that the creditors and donor countries should put their priorities right in their policy regarding development cooperation in educational matters. While clearly no country in need should be denied international assistance, priority should be given to developing countries.[364] The findings of the Special Rapporteur on the right to education reveal the need for another policy priority for donor States in this regard. They should in the first place allocate resources and technical assistance in order to realise those aspects that belong to the core content of the right

---

[360] Article 11 of the Dakar Framework for Action, adopted in 2000 in Dakar (Senegal), *o.c.* (note 42), p. 9.

[361] CRC Committee, *General Comment No. 5: General measures of implementation of the Convention on the Rights of the Child* (UN Doc. CRC/GC/2003/5, 2003), para. 62.

[362] K. Tomaševski, *Progress Report of the Special Rapporteur on the Right to Education 1999/25* (UN Doc. E/CN.4/2000/6, 2000), paras. 14 and 22; K. Tomaševski, *Annual Report of the Special Rapporteur on the Right to Education 2000/9* (UN Doc. E/CN.4/2001/52, 2001), paras. 51–54; K. Tomaševski, *Annual Report of the Special Rapporteur on the Right to Education 2001/29* (UN Doc. E/CN.4/2002/60, 2002), paras. 17–18; K. Tomaševski, *Annual Report of the special Rapporteur on the Right to Education 2002/23* (UN Doc. E/CN.4/2003/9, 2003), para. 11; and K. Tomaševski, *Education Denied*, *o.c.* (note 53), 133–141.

[363] K. Annan, *We the Children, Meeting the promises of the World Summit for Children*, *o.c.* (note 52), p. 70.

[364] This is confirmed in Article 14 of the Dakar Framework for Action, adopted in 2000 in Dakar (Senegal), *o.c.* (note 42), p. 9.

to education, such as the realisation of free and compulsory primary education and the realisation of special facilities for persons with an educational deficit (*cf. supra* No. 42).[365]

As already stated above, the term 'international cooperation' not only refers to bilateral cooperation but also to cooperation by States as members of intergovernmental organisations. Both the CRC Committee and the CESCR Committee maintain that States Parties have an obligation to ensure that their actions as members of international organizations, take due account of the right to education.[366] In this context, in particular the role of international financial institutions (the World Bank, the International Monetary Fund, and the regional development banks) is stressed in the sense that they should have a human rights oriented approach to structural adjustment programmes and debt relief initiatives.[367] This has also been a recurring concern of the Special Rapporteur on the Right to Education.[368]

[365] K. Tomaševski, *Progress Report of the Special Rapporteur on the Right to Education 1999/25* (UN Doc. E/CN.4/2000/6, 2000), para. 15.

[366] CRC Committee, *General Comment No. 5: General measures of implementation of the Convention on the Rights of the Child* (UN Doc. CRC/GC/2003/5, 2003), paras. 63–64; CESCR Committee, *General Comment No. 13 on the Right to Education* (UN Doc. E/C.12/1999/10, 1999), para. 56. See also See K. Tomaševski, *The Right to education, Annual Report of the Special Rapporteur on the right to education 2003* (UN Doc. E/CN.4/2004/45, 2004), para. 16.

[367] CRC Committee, *General Comment No. 5: General measures of implementation of the Convention on the Rights of the Child* (UN Doc. CRC/GC/2003/5, 2003), paras. 62 and 64; CESCR Committee, *General Comment No. 13 on the Right to Education* (UN Doc. E/C.12/1999/10, 1999), para. 60.

[368] K. Tomaševski, *Progress Report of the Special Rapporteur on the Right to Education 1999/25* (UN Doc. E/CN.4/2000/6, 2000), paras. 23–29; K. Tomaševski, *Annual Report of the Special Rapporteur on the Right to Education 2000/9* (UN Doc. E/CN.4/2001/52, 2001), paras. 31–41; K. Tomaševski, *Annual Report of the Special Rapporteur on the Right to Education 2001/29* (UN Doc. E/CN.4/2002/60, 2002), paras. 14–16; K. Tomaševski, *Annual Report of the special Rapporteur on the Right to Education 2002/23* (UN Doc. E/CN.4/2003/9, 2003), paras. 9 and 13; and K. Tomaševski, *Education Denied*, *o.c.* (note 53), pp. 69–82.

www.ingramcontent.com/pod-product-compliance
Lightning Source LLC
LaVergne TN
LVHW092341011026
849160LV00022B/98

* 9 7 8 9 0 0 4 1 4 7 2 9 4 *